LEAVING YOUR LEADERSHIP LEGACY

Also by the Authors

Buried Alive!
Digging Out of a Management Dumpster

Confessions of an UnManager
Ten Steps to Jump Start Company
Performance by Getting Others
to Accept Accountability

LEAVING YOUR LEADERSHIP LEGACY

CREATING A TIMELESS AND ENDURING CULTURE OF CLARITY, CONNECTIVITY AND CONSISTENCY

BY

SHANE A. YOUNT

WITH JOHN PYECHA,
DEBRA BOGGAN, ANNA VERSTEEG
AND LINDA SEGALL

RICHMOND, VIRGINIA

ISBN 10: 1-892538-42-3
ISBN 13: 978-1-892538-42-0

If your bookseller does not have this book in stock, it can be ordered directly from the publisher. Contact us for information about discounts on quantity purchases.

The Oaklea Press
6912 Three Chopt Road, Suite B
Richmond, Virginia 23226

Voice: 1-800-295-4066
Facsimile: 1-804-281-5686
Email: Info@OakleaPress.com

This book can be purchased online at

http://www.LeanTransformation.com

CONTENTS

Chapter 1: The Decision

Ima Manijer sat shivering in the city hospital emergency room. She got up to put another warm blanket on her mother as they both waited for the ER doctor to come back with test results.

"It's so cold in here," her mother whispered. "Why do they keep it so cold in here?"

"I don't know, Mom," she replied, wishing she'd brought a sweater with her. She should have known better. Ima was (unfortunately) experienced in knowing what to expect in the ER. This was the third time in six months that she had brought her 90 year old mother here.

It was always a long wait. And it was always cold.

Thankfully, none of the situations that had taken them to the hospital had been life-threatening, although they had been urgent. (This time, her mother was suffering from some type of flu, and the family doctor didn't want to take a chance on dehydration. On a previous visit, she had fallen and needed x-rays to rule out a broken ankle. And the first time, she had suffered mysterious chest pains that the doctors never could diagnose.)

Ima fitfully looked at her watch: It was 1 a.m. They had been in the ER for three hours, and it looked as if it would be another hour or two before the doctor would either discharge her mother or admit her for observation. She wouldn't get any sleep tonight, and that was bad, because she had an important meeting at 7 a.m. at the plant.

I'm getting too old for this, Ima said to herself. *I just don't have the energy or stamina to do everything I did when I was 40 or even 50 years old.* Ima was in her mid 60s.

If she'd spoken those thoughts out loud, a passerby might have thought Ima to be bitter about being her mother's caregiver. She wasn't. Her mother had spent the first 18 years of Ima's life taking care of and raising her, and now it was Ima's turn to take care of her mother. But she occasionally allowed herself a moment of self-pity, because the demands were starting to get to her.

Three years ago, Ima's mother asked if she could come live with her. "It's time," she'd said. And it was time. Her widowed mother was too frail to live alone. But the living arrangement put an even greater burden on Ima.

The responsibility for chauffeuring her mother to multiple doctors' appointments (sometimes two or three a week), taking her to the beauty shop, and being awakened at midnight to scurry to the ER fell on her shoulders, no one else's.

When do I get some time for myself? Ima asked herself. *There's so much I want to do, but I just don't have the time.*

Ima was manager of the Eniware Manufacturing Plant, where she'd spent most of her career. The job was demanding yet fulfilling. It hadn't always been that way, though. She remembered several years ago when she had been *Buried Alive!* in her personal management dumpster.

At that time, as a team leader, she felt that she couldn't get *anything* done, because every day more and more seemed to be dumped on her by everyone — top management, her peers, her employees. She was so mired down that she dreaded going to work each morning.

Then, one day when she was at the depth of her despair — buried alive, so to speak — her colleague Tim Leder came to her rescue.

Tim was at the time Ima's opposite. Whereas Ima

8

dreaded going to work in the morning, hated dealing with employees, and no longer enjoyed the work she performed, Tim loved everything about his job. When he got up in the morning, he could hardly wait to get to the plant. And why not? Going to work wasn't a vacation, but it wasn't stressful, either. Tim found that work gave him a great sense of satisfaction. That was because Tim's team had things under control. Most of the time, everything went right, according to plan. And when it didn't, the team figured out what to do and got back on track.

Back in those days, a casual observer would never have guessed that Ima and Tim had developed as managers in the same plant. Ima looked haggard and depressed, mired down by the weight of her work. She viewed work pessimistically, convinced that she could never get everything done. Tim was Mr. Energy, an optimist full of enthusiasm for what could be accomplished that day. He was energetic and all smiles.

What made the difference between the two of them was a secret Tim had discovered: He had found a path that had led him out of *his* dumpster. Ima had not — until Tim came along.

That fateful day, Tim had given her the tools to build steps upward and out of her dumpster. He had guided her into understanding how to manage *smarter*, by developing a true sense of focus, urgency, and accountability among her employees. And it wasn't just the spirit of teamwork that so many "flavor-of-the-month" programs had touted previously. No, she thought, what Tim had taught her was the *real* thing, based on a sense of responsibility that everyone felt and accepted and cemented in real communication.

That climb had been the beginning of a new life for her.

Now here she was, pushing 65 and plant manager! The plant had done well under her direction; her life was good. But the plant also took her time — a lot of it.

Ima's mother began to complain again. "Where is that doctor? Why does it take so long to get anything done in this hospital?" she moaned and again complained that she was cold.

Ima went to the warming cabinet and took out a blanket. As she tucked the blanket in, her mother said, "You know what this place needs, Ima?"

"You mean in addition to a new thermostat?" Ima smiled.

"It certainly could use that!" her mother replied. "But what it *really* needs is someone like you to run it. I mean, there is really no reason why we should have to wait so long — and have to shiver while we're waiting. Why, you *should* be running it!"

"I'm not a hospital administrator, Mom," said Ima. "I wouldn't know the first thing about running a hospital."

"No. But you didn't know anything about working with the city when that blizzard happened last year. But you got the mayor out of a real mess!" her mother exclaimed proudly.

"I just volunteered to help," said Ima.

"You know it was a lot more than that," insisted her mother. "Just volunteering wouldn't have gotten you the key to the city and that nice plaque from the mayor. What did it say, something like, 'To Ima Manijir, who turned chaos aside and in its place put the best-run volunteer emergency disaster team this city has ever known."

"Mom! You're exaggerating!" Ima exclaimed modestly as she tucked the blanket around her mother. "I really didn't do anything so special."

But she had.

The year before, a freak snowstorm had turned into a history-making blizzard and caught the community off guard. The wind blew ferociously, and snow fell relentlessly. Power lines went down. The few snowplows the city owned couldn't keep the main roads cleared.

Ima, like everyone else in town, watched the weather forecast and eyed the blowing snow as it banked higher and higher on the streets. The television showed hundreds (maybe thousands!) of abandoned cars and people who were desperate to get home and take care of their families. The dark city was effectively shut down. It was a disaster; yet she saw little being done to fix a problem that kept getting worse by the minute. The only thing the mayor seemed to be doing was putting in calls to the National Guard for help.

The city was outside the traditional northern snow belt, so it didn't have a fleet of snowplows. The mayor was not prepared to deal with this life-threatening situation.

With the blizzard predicted to continue for at least 24 hours and the temperature plummeting, Ima decided she had to try to help. She called the mayor.

"Mr. Mayor," she pleaded, "We have to do something. What is your plan to help all of those people who can't get home and who don't have any heat or electricity?"

"I don't know, Ima," he whined sorrowfully. "I called the governor to ask for the National Guard to be sent in. Help will be coming; we just don't know when. ... We just weren't prepared for this. I mean ... this is the blizzard of the century! No one saw it coming."

"I know that," said Ima. "But we have to deal with it

now. We can't wait for the National Guard. People are stranded. They don't have food, water, heat, or electricity. I want to help. Let's see if we can get your people and a bunch of volunteers to collaborate and get us through this mess."

Ima scanned through her PDA as she talked with the mayor. She identified a number of top managers in companies that used heavy equipment. Within minutes, she organized a conference call as the first step in mobilizing a small team of city officials and top managers from the city's major companies.

Modeled after teams that Ima had successfully built in her plant, the city's first cooperative disaster-management team went into action. It quickly marshalled its collective resources, cascaded the team effort downward into smaller sections of the city, and saved the city and its residents from what could have been its worst disaster ever.

Within an hour, using heavy equipment lent by area companies, shifts of volunteers began working to clear streets, move abandoned cars and relocate people without heat, electricity, food or water to hastily opened community shelters, manned by still more volunteers. By the time the National Guard plowed its way to the city line, the city's residents were safe and sound.

The best part of that experience, thought Ima, was that the city would never be caught off guard again, because the disaster teams had maintained themselves. They met regularly, and team members planned for what would be needed in terms of people and resources for all types of emergencies — floods, fires, tornadoes, blizzards. After getting them organized, Ima bowed out of the limelight, but the teams kept convening "Ima meetings" (as they called them), and the city was now prepared for whatever Mother Nature threw at them.

And that's why Ima had received the key to the city and the plaque from the mayor.

Ima wasn't about to argue with her mother about her role in the blizzard, so she changed the subject. "I got an e-mail from Jennifer today," she said. "She sent pictures of the kids. Gosh, I wish I could see them! They're growing up so fast."

Jennifer was Ima's daughter, who lived a 1,000 miles away. The kids were two of Ima's grandchildren, ages seven and three. Her other two grandchildren (who were even younger) lived closer — 500 miles — but still too far for her to see them very often.

"Why don't you go visit them when I get over this flu, Ima? I'll be OK," said her mother.

"I know ... but it's hard. I have so much work and so little time!"

So little time. *It's funny how fast time goes the older you get, she thought. And it's time I can never get back. If only I didn't have all these daily responsibilities, I could do things on my own schedule instead of someone else's...*

"You know, Ima, you could have plenty of time. You're going to be 65 in six months. Why don't you retire? You've done your part. In fact, you've done a great job. Give yourself the gift of time, before you don't have it anymore."

Ima looked at her mother and silently repeated what she had said: *The gift of time.* Then she smiled at her mother. "When did you get so wise?" she asked with a tease.

Then she whispered, almost to herself, "You've given me something to think about."

Lesson 1: Leadership and the Management Dumpster

A dumpster, by definition, is a commercial trash and garbage receptacle found behind most businesses. In it are placed the discards from the day's work: paper, printouts, trash of all sorts. Most dumpsters are steel bins that have sloping sides and metal tops heavy enough to keep stuff from blowing out.

Commercial dumpsters serve a valuable purpose: They're where people get rid of "stuff." And as long as they're emptied regularly so that they don't overflow, they serve their purpose well.

But when they're not emptied regularly, they become home and haven to all sorts of vermin and health hazards.

A management dumpster is the emotional equivalent of the commercial variety. It's an emotional and mental trash bin for managers. It stores the complaints, problems, obsolete programs and, most important, the inappropriate accountabilities of employees, customers, co-workers and even bosses. A management dumpster is a mental and emotional health hazard to the work environment.

Leaders can have their own personal management dumpsters. They make daily to-do lists but never get anything accomplished. Their good intentions to build attitudes of collaboration and consensus, which (they believe) will result in accountability, create a culture of dependency instead. Their teams depend on them to make decisions instead of holding the team and its members accountable to do "the next right thing."

Leaders who find themselves deep into this vicious circle of accountability feel buried alive in the bottom of a management dumpster, because they lack time to do each day for others what those others could do for themselves.

If you're a manager who's fallen into a management dumpster, you may view work as a chore and challenges as insurmountable obstacles. You no longer take joy in going to work. Instead, every day is "Monday," and you feel that you have a never-ending to-do list.

Often, managers who fall into their dumpsters think that if they leave their current job and find another, things will get better. The sad fact is, things rarely do. Instead, the managers take empty dumpsters with them to the next job, then fill them up again in a never-ending cycle.

This happens because of the paradigm of leadership by which they manage. This faulty paradigm causes them to:

• Operate without focus, urgency, and accountability;

• Rely on personalities (their own, plus the personalities of "key" employees) instead of business processes to achieve results; and

• Fail to elevate expectations of engagement.

Leaders who find themselves in a management dumpster often recognize their dilemma and try to climb out by applying a quick fix. They may try to change the organization by implementing new structures (such as formal teams) or imposing new programs (such as operational excellence or lean manufacturing).

Or, given some insights, they may attempt to change *themselves* by emulating what they believe are successful management traits.

Noble as they are, these attempts are doomed to failure, because each is essentially a band-aid solution to the problem.

In other words, the solution to climbing out of a management dumpster and leading the organization to sustainable success can be accomplished only by addressing the problem as a whole. That requires putting a new leadership paradigm into place – one based on non-negotiable processes that elevate expectations of engagement through core systems of accountability and communication.

In a nutshell, the solution requires transforming yourself into a principled leader who does *not* rely on *position* (that is, your title and authority), powers of *persuasion* or *proximity* to the team to achieve results. Rather, the solution relies on the power of non-negotiable processes to achieve a culture of *clarity, consistency,* and *connectivity.*

Self-Assessment 1: Are You in a Management Dumpster?

Answer the following questions to determine if you are in a management dumpster:

1. Look at your to-do list from yesterday. How many of the items did you manage to cross off? Were they important? Urgent? Look back on your to-do lists from the previous week: Were you able to cross off most of the tasks every day? What kinds of tasks carried over, day after day? Do you find yourself frustrated that you cannot accomplish the things you think are most important?

2. Do you find yourself being the victim of "drive-bys" or "hit-and-runs" (those urgent requests from employees, colleagues, or your boss that begin with "Can you do ..." and "You need to ...")?

3. Do you find yourself taking care of issues or concerns that others should be able to take care of themselves?

4. Think about the group of employees you supervise. Whom do you rely on most? Do you feel that every employee is equally responsible and dependable to get the work done – even those "extra" things that seem to crop up every day? Or do you have a selective engagement within your team – that is, do you pick on certain employees you know will come through instead of expecting all employees to do their share? Why do you think this happens?

5. Do you feel you are mostly accountable for the results of the organization?

6. Think again about the employees you supervise: When a task is left undone or a project unfinished, do your employees point to "ignorance as an excuse" for not doing what needs to be done?

7. Is it a struggle to create a sense of urgency within your team?

8. Do you have to persuade your employees to do their jobs or to do anything "extra"?

9. Do you feel more confident that work is being done when you're in the area, than when you're away from it?

10. Think about the various quality-improvement, productivity-improvement, and morale-building programs you've put into place throughout your career. Did these programs achieve the results they were supposed to? How sustained were the results they did achieve? Are you satisfied with those results?

11. Do you find yourself thinking, *If only I were higher up on the management chain, then I wouldn't have these problems?*

Comment:

No matter where you are in the management chain — at the lowest level or at the highest, leadership comes with its share of frustrations. But if those frustrations build up and cause you to feel helpless to meet your goals, you may be in a management dumpster.

But you can climb out — if you put into place self-sustaining business processes based on clarity, consistency, and connectivity.

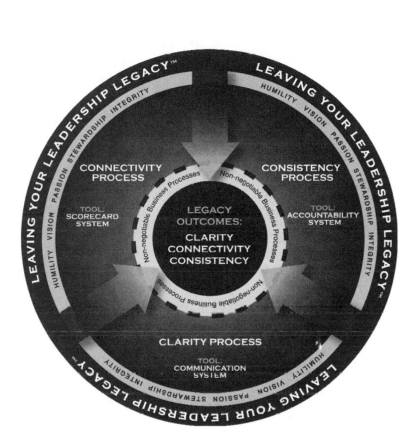

Chapter 2: Doubts

Ima sat at her desk in the Eniware Manufacturing Plant, fiddling with a few papers. She swiveled her chair around twice, stopped it in front of the computer, and idly ran her fingers across the keyboard.

She shuffled some folders, arranged a pen and pencil perpendicular to the edge of the desk and pushed her coffee mug an inch to the right. Then she got up and walked around the office's inside perimeter.

She stopped in front of the picture window that looked out over the expanse of the plant and its many buildings. It was about 3 p.m., and a shift was changing, so there was little "work" going on. Team members, though, were congregating in small groups.

From the distance, it looked as if they were socializing, but Ima knew better. They were exchanging information in "business huddles." Team members finishing the day shift were updating those clocking in for the afternoon shift, telling the newcomers about their team's scorecard performance and sharing the status of their shift action registers so that everyone knew what had been done and what needed to be done during the shift. They were also passing down critical information from the primary team headed by Ima, the plant manager. The result was that everyone was "in the know."

These 10-minute business huddles were a non-negotiable standard operating procedure throughout the plant.

Because it was shift change, only a few forklifts could be seen darting in and out of the various buildings. In the near distance, almost directly below her window, Ima spied a small group of employees flagging down a forklift operator. Of course, Ima couldn't hear what they were saying, but she saw the operator absently touch his face, nod to the others and reach into his pocket for his safety glasses. He thanked them for their concern.

That's what I like to see, thought Ima. *Everyone looking out for the plant and each other.*

Soon none of this would be her responsibility. Thirty-two years. That's how long she'd been part of this plant. She had started as a young supervisor. Now she was finishing her career as the plant manager. A long time, she thought.

But if the last 32 years of working in the Eniware plant had gone by fast, the last six months since her decision to retire had gone even faster. She was literally within hours of turning over the keys of the plant to her replacement, who was coming to the Eniware plant from another of the company's facilities.

Ima had hoped that the company president would appoint someone from her own management team to take over, but this was not the case. There would be other opportunities for Ima's team members. This time, the new plant manager was coming from a sister plant, where he'd managed the supply chain. Ima expected him tomorrow. She'd take a few days to help him get settled, and then she would leave.

It was a bittersweet time for her. She'd worked hard and was looking forward to retirement. *I'll miss all this,* thought Ima. *But I'll have my memories. And I have so much more I want to do – travel, take care of Mom, see the grandkids. Maybe I'll even play some golf!* She smiled to herself as she envisioned herself chasing a little white ball around a golf course.

If Ima were honest with herself, she would admit that this "self-talk" was mostly bravado. Yes, retirement was alluring, but she was concerned about the plant's future. Would everything she had worked so hard to accomplish vanish when she closed the door behind her? What if her replacement didn't do things as she had done? What if …

A quick rap at the door broke into Ima's thoughts.

"Hey, lady!" Tim Leder said, as he announced himself with a smile. "How's the woman-of-almost-leisure?"

Just as Ima's career had progressed because of the great job she'd done, so had Tim's. When Tim had coached Ima out of her management dumpster, he, like Ima, had been a team leader. Now he was vice president of North American operations.

The position hadn't gone to his head, though. He was still a caring individual, a wonderful teacher, and – most of all – an example of humility amid so many personal accomplishments. And although he was Ima's boss, Tim was also Ima's friend and mentor.

Ima turned toward the sound of Tim's effervescent voice. "Hi, Tim! You caught me doing a little daydreaming. … I can't believe that I'll be saying good-bye to all this in just a few more days. As much as I'm looking forward to being that 'woman of leisure' as you put it, I'm going to miss everyone and everything."

She sighed audibly as she stared out onto the plant below, again absorbed in thought and concern. Then she snapped out of her daydream and asked, "What brings you here today? I didn't think I'd see you until tomorrow, when the new guy arrives."

Tim often showed up unannounced. They frequently popped into one another's office without notice, just to talk as well as to bounce ideas off each other. So, Ima wasn't surprised by his visit.

"I just needed to get a dose of envy, watching you pack up your stuff and listen to you talk about all the things you're going to do once you no longer have to wake up to the alarm clock! What's the first thing you're going to do as a retired woman?"

"I'll be busy enough," replied Ima. "After I catch up on my sleep for a couple of days, I plan to do some traveling and see my grandkids. Fortunately, my mother is feeling well, so I'm going to take her along. It'll be nice to take a long vacation without having to worry about hurrying home." Ima had a smile on her face, but her expression was flat.

"And then?" asked Tim, who noticed that Ima's voice lacked the enthusiasm he had expected.

"And then ..." Ima had turned toward the window again and didn't finish the sentence.

"Ima, you're not regretting your decision, are you?" asked Tim.

"No ... but I *will* miss everyone," she admitted. "It's not as easy letting go as I thought it would be... I once read that everyone is temporary. It's like sticking your finger in a bucket of water and taking it out. At first there's a ripple, but then, it's like the finger was never there. Is that what it's going to be like around here? Like I had never been here?"

"Ima, everyone may be temporary, but the things they leave behind can live on forever — provided they're the right things." said Tim. "And you are leaving the right things. Just look around you."

He walked over to the window. "Look at what's going

on down there … the teamwork. The focus of your employees. That can't go away. It's part of the Eniware plant now. You did this. It's your leadership legacy."

"I don't know, Tim. Everyone really can be replaced. I mean … I've seen it over the years. Good employees leave for another job. Or they retire. Or they die. We miss them, but life goes on. We find someone to take their place. And that's what's happening to me, too. Tomorrow there will be someone new."

"That's right, Ima. Life goes on, and tomorrow there will be someone new. But that doesn't mean your legacy doesn't live on forever."

"My legacy? What legacy?" cried Ima. "I'm just a person who did her job. And now it's over."

Lesson 2: A Leadership Legacy

A legacy is something that is handed down – bequeathed, as it were, to future generations. If it is a true legacy, it lives on forever.

True legacies – things handed down from the past – are not created in a moment. They take time to build.

Consider, for example, inheritances – one type of legacy. What is an average 21-year-old's monetary worth? How much money do you think he (or she) has in the bank? How many investments does he hold? What is the sum total of all of his assets?

The average 21-year-old isn't worth too much, but his *potential* worth is considerable. With discipline and a process to save and invest, at the end of his career he can be in a position to leave an inheritance, accumulated over time, to his heirs – provided he starts *now*.

The legacy of leadership works in much the same way. Your leadership legacy is what you would leave behind if you left your organization today.

If you define your legacy solely in terms of accomplishments, your "heirs" will squander it fast, because whatever accomplishments are, they can be (and will be) outdone by your successor – just as *yours* surpassed your predecessor's!

But it you build your legacy over time through *discipline and processes,* it will last forever. The memories you create, the methods you use, and the values you instill in your organization form a foundation for an organization with three unmistakable elements: connectivity, clarity, and consistency.

More on this later.

Self-Assessment 2: What Kind of Legacy Will You Leave?

Answer these questions with total honesty:

1. What is more important to you: the *results* you achieve or how you achieve them?

2. Have you made the impact you wanted to make in your work?

3. Will your employees remember you as someone who made a difference in their lives?

4. When you are gone, will you leave your "mark" on the organization? How?

5. Will the values you instilled and lived by endure long after you have left?

6. Have you put into place a system that will enable your employees to feel a sense of clarity – that is, a communication process that gives each individual the knowledge and information he or she needs to be effective?

7. Have you implemented a system to give your employees a feeling of being connected with the business – that is, a system in which they know if they are winning or losing and how to respond in their work accordingly?

8. Have you left an operating system that is not dependent on *you* to give your employees what they

Comment:

Experts in communication tell us, "It is not what you say so much as how you say it." The same is true in leadership: Results are important, but so is how you achieve them.

Some managers focus only on results at the expense of everything (and everyone) else in the organization. Other managers go to the other extreme and rely on the energy of their charisma to realize accomplishments.

Leadership is not an either/or characteristic. What you want to strive for as part of your legacy is a balance between the "what" and the "how." This balance will not only help you achieve the impact you desire, it will also cause your employees to remember you in the way you wish to be remembered.

Either/or leaders leave behind memories. Memories are important, but in the business world, so are results – *sustainable* results. You can achieve these results by putting into place processes that allow employees to clearly understand their roles in achieving success and their connection with the business.

Chapter 3: A Matter of Position

Tim had known Ima for a long time. And he knew that tone of voice. It wouldn't make any difference how hard he argued; he would not be able to convince her that she would not be forgotten – that she was, indeed, leaving a legacy.

So instead of arguing, he wandered around the office, looking at the things she was leaving behind. He stopped by the bookcase.

"Hey … aren't you going to pack this?" he asked. He turned around, holding a dusty scrapbook.

"That? No. That album belongs to the plant. I found it here when I inherited this office, so I'll leave it for my successor. I think it's a history of the plant."

"Really? Come on … let's take a look! One last time to walk down memory lane," Tim suggested. Before she could protest, he sat down, pulled out a chair for her next to him and opened the book.

The Eniware plant had been built in the early 1960s, years before either of them had come to work there. On the first page of the scrapbook, a faded newspaper article made known the company's intention to locate in Eniware and hire several hundred employees. Another yellowed newspaper piece reported a ground-breaking ceremony, attended by the mayor of the town, a number of city council members, and VIPs from corporate headquarters.

Black-and-white photographs showed the first managers and a number of the newly hired employees performing various jobs around the plant. Other photos took a "tour" of the new facility and pointed out the type of work done in each department.

The plant had changed over the years with the addition of new buildings and modern, computer-assisted machines and robots, but Tim and Ima could recognize some of the equipment and buildings still in use today.

As Tim flipped through the pages; they both laughed at some of the pictures with dates from the late 1960s. "Look at that ... those sideburns! I hate to admit it, but back then I had that same kind of shaggy haircut," said Tim.

Ima laughed, too. "Some of those haircuts are really bad! And look at the clothes the women are wearing! Skirts, hose, and high heels, and those high beehive hair-dos. You can bet those women weren't working on the plant floor."

"No, not in those days. If I remember right, it wasn't until the mid '70s that women really began to be an accept-ed part of the factory workforce, other than in support positions like clerks and secretaries. 'You've come a long way, baby!'" Tim teased.

They continued turning pages, looking for familiar scenes and laughing at old technology. Every page they turned brought them closer to when each had been hired.

"Hey, look at this!" exclaimed Tim. "Isn't that you?"

Ima peered at the small black-and-white photo. In it, she was standing at attention with a group of about a dozen men, all dressed in white shirts and ties and wearing white hard hats, somberly posing for the photographer. The photo was captioned, "Managers and Supervisors."

"I'd forgotten about that photo! That was taken shortly after I was hired. Look how young I was then!"

"When did you come to work here, Ima?" Tim asked.

"It was in June 1975. I was 33 years old," Ima recalled.

She got caught up in the memory. "When I graduated from high school, I went to work in an auto assembly plant. They were beginning to hire women then, and it was good money. At that time, I didn't think I wanted to go to college.

"Several years after I started working on the assembly line, though, I decided I wanted to get into management. I knew I wanted to become a decision-maker, not just a doer. So, I enrolled in night school and worked on my college degree part-time. It took me about eight years, juggling working full-time and raising my daughter and son, but I finally graduated with a degree in business administration. Unfortunately, the plant where I was working was only willing to hire women for the assembly line, not in management. That's changed today, of course, but when I was ready to step up, there weren't any opportunities there. So, I started looking around. I applied at the Eniware plant and the plant manager – that fellow standing next to me in the picture – was willing to hire me as the plant's first female supervisor," she said with a hint of pride.

"That's really cool, and obviously they made the right decision! Being the 'first' had to have been challenging, though. But then, I suppose they put you through all kinds of supervisory training programs to make sure you'd succeed."

"Training?" exclaimed Ima. "You've got to be kidding! No one got training in those days. I was grateful to be hired! The only 'training' I received was to watch older supervisors, figure out what seemed to work for *them*, and then try it myself."

"That's a hard way to learn, a trial by fire," Tim reflected. "If you don't model yourself after the right people, you can make a lot of mistakes."

"I guess so. I tried to model myself after my department manager, who used the plant manager as *his* model. It *seemed* to work."

Tim didn't comment, and they were silent for a few minutes as he turned a couple more pages.

A photo finally caught his attention. "I guess people didn't have enough to do back then."

The picture showed several employees working in the foreground, but in the background, almost out of the camera's eye and slightly blurred, were a number of other workers, sitting around a makeshift table, playing cards.

Ima peered at the photo closely. "Oh, my gosh. I don't believe it. This picture was taken in my department when I was a brand new supervisor! I remember some of those guys ... It was tough getting them to do their work."

"How so?"

"Employees back then had an attitude that they would do *only* what was required. I mean ... they had basic work to do – like production quotas for the day. But when they got it done, they wouldn't do anything else unless they were told to. And even then, they might say, 'It's not in my job description.' So, if they did their 'job' in six hours instead of eight, they felt like they could sit around the breakroom until it was time to clock out.

"I'm sure that didn't go over big with you or with your plant manager. How did you handle it?"

"Well, I told you we didn't get any supervisory training. I figured my best bet would be to model myself after supervisors I had known. And most of them got work out of their employees by threatening them. So, that's what I did. If I gave an assignment and the crew balked at doing it, I used my authority. You know ... 'I'm the boss. Take my road or the high road!' "

"How did that work out?" asked Tim.

Ima thought for a moment. "Well, you know how people are. They create an environment of fear for themselves. Or, perhaps it would be more accurate to say they're afraid to lose their jobs, especially when jobs are scarce. So when I resorted to those tactics, work got done. But I could never rely on them to go beyond the basics ... you know, to take on the next project or do the 'little things' like cleanup without being told."

"So, if I'm hearing you right, you used your *position* to get the job done. But it didn't have a long-term effect," observed Tim. "It sounds that despite power-wielding, employees weren't held accountable for doing more than 'just their jobs.' It sounds like they really didn't buy into the fact that 'those extra things' really were part of their job, and all those tasks contributed to the company's success, one way or another."

Ima thought for a minute. "Yes, that's right. That's how it was back then."

"Back then, but not now," emphasized Tim.

"No, not now," Ima mused. She turned the page but didn't catch the meaning of what Tim was getting at.

Lesson 3: Managing by Position

Leaders can be powerful people. In formal structures, their power is conveyed through title and authority. In other words, if you have the title of supervisor, manager, director, vice president, president or other designation, you have been given authority because of the position you hold.

Traditionally, leaders use their titles and authority – their positions – to achieve results: They set policy, give direction and make decisions which they expect others will execute.

Although this type of leadership achieves results, those results are fleeting, because they are totally dependent upon the leader's position. If the leader "goes away" – that is, if his or her title is removed – the organization flounders until someone else is appointed.

Title and authority are not "bad" things. Every organization has them. But if the organization defines its leadership in terms of position and authority and not processes, then it will not be able to sustain success over the long haul.

Self-Assessment 3: Do You Lead by Position?

1. Are you copied on endless e-mails because people are afraid to leave you out of the loop or because they know that if you are copied, others will respond?

2. Does the tone of meetings vary, depending on the level of individuals who shows up?

3. If meetings take place when you are not there, are they effective? Are decisions made in your absence?

4. Does it take your personal endorsement to get things done?

5. Do people loiter around your office in the hope of getting a few minutes of your time because they are afraid to move forward without your being "in the loop?"

6. Does your calendar stay full with appointments with people who vie for your time and approval?

7. Do people wait to see your reaction before expressing their opinions?

8. When you give an opinion, do your subordinates rephrase their position to be in line with your thinking?

Comment:

Don't let the influence that your title and authority convey to you go to your head. When employees describe the traits they value in leaders, they pick humility as the single most important quality that motivates them. The feelings of self-importance that come from overfilled calendars and constant demands on your time are intoxicating, but remember that intoxication can produce a hangover and a splitting headache.

In the case of "position intoxication," the hangover is

an organization without accountability, urgency and a business focus. The headache is a management dumpster.

The solution is simple: Put into place Process-Based Leadership™ that does not rely on your position to achieve results.

Chapter 4: Pointless Persuasion

They flipped through several more pages of the scrapbook until they came to what appeared to be a group picture of Ima's entire department. The formality of the photo was marred by one individual who made a "face" in front of the camera.

"What the …?" said Tim, looking at the photo closely. "Isn't that Monk E. Onurbak? Why the devil would he want to ruin the picture like a six-year-old?"

Ima peered at the photo and sighed. "Yes, that's Monk. Good ole Monk. He was always trying to get away with something. And he usually succeeded, just like he did in this picture. I'm sure he wasn't thinking the picture would be around 30 years later. He was just trying to be funny. Only most of the time, his sense of humor left a lot to be desired."

Tim remembered Monk well. The day he'd rescued Ima from her management dumpster, Monk had been bullying her to do something for him.

"Hey, Ima," Tim remembered Monk yelling. "Wait up. I gotta talk to you. … It's my paycheck. You gotta do something about it. They shorted me four hours of overtime. I work, I wanna be paid. You owe me! Do something about it."

That was the way Monk talked to everyone, no exception for supervisors. He was a big fellow, more than six feet tall and burly. Because he was big and loud, he easily intimidated everyone around him.

"Monk always was a handful to manage, wasn't he," Tim recalled.

"That's an understatement." Ima remembered the frustration she would feel whenever she had to deal with Monk and several others who were his good friends.

She lowered her voice to almost a whisper and confessed, "I never told this to anyone, but in the early days, Monk drove me to the edge more than once. Even using my position on him had minimal results. He did the minimum – enough to frustrate me, but not enough for me to write him up. I found myself giving him an order, and then I would get off the shop floor and back to my office as quickly as I could, because I didn't want to see if he did what I told him or not. If he didn't, I would have to confront him, and some days, I just couldn't handle it.

"I remember one day in particular ... I was so frustrated I was on the verge of tears. I stomped into my manager's office and told him I couldn't take it any more."

"What did he do?" asked Tim.

"He told me to be nice."

"What?"

"Yep, that's what he said. I remember him telling me, 'Don't try to tell Monk anything. Just be nice to him. Remember: You can catch more flies with honey than you can with vinegar!'

"That was all he said. But that wasn't what I wanted to hear. I wanted a solution, and he gave me a platitude! How could I be *nice* to an employee who was bent on making my life miserable?

"But as I calmed down, I thought about what my manager had advised. He didn't tell me what I wanted to hear, but maybe his advice had some merit. I mean ... I remembered all the different supervisors I had had during my years working on the assembly line. I had always had a good work ethic, but when I had a supervisor I liked and who was nice to me, even I put in extra effort. But when I had a supervisor who barked orders, I didn't feel like bending over backwards. Sure, I did my job, because that's what I do, but I resented the harsh treatment.

"So, I thought about how to be *nice*. My first attempts were to smile and ask if Monk and his friends would 'please' do this or that."

"And what happened? Did it work?" asked Tim.

"Nope. After 'pleasing' those guys, I would end up ordering them – resorting to using my power card. And my frustration mounted."

"Did you go back to your boss and ask for help?"

"Yes. He said, 'Being nice doesn't just mean saying "please." It means persuading them to do what you want them to do. You know … find out what's important to them, and negotiate: They get what *they* want, and you get what *you* want.'

"He was so sure that this would solve the problem that he even sent me to one of those seminars on how to influence people. I remember the instructor talking about each employee's proverbial 'happy meter' … a kind of gas tank. 'Keep those happy meters full,' he said, 'and life will be good!' And how are you supposed to keep the tanks full? By being nice, by doing things for them. By being an enabler."

"How did it work out for you?" asked Tim.

Ima laughed. "I think my employees liked me more! But as far as getting the job done … well, sometimes it was OK; often, not. Most of the time when I used my charm and convinced them what had to be done, the crew did what I asked them to do. But they rarely would act on their own. It was more like they were doing me a personal favor than they were doing it because that was the right thing to do. I kept waiting for this personal epiphany that the consultants said would happen one day, but, needless to say, it never did. I wore myself out trying to persuade people to work!"

"Was it like that with all your employees, or just Monk and his friends?"

"Some workers were better than others. They really did like me, and they didn't want to get me in trouble for not meeting standards or for missing quality specifications. I think deep down they were afraid they'd get someone worse if I were replaced!" she laughed.

"And if you were replaced, then they'd go back to their old habits unless the new guy convinced them otherwise," said Tim.

"Yes … back to their old habits of doing only what needed to be done to keep their jobs, with no ownership of what had to be done to make Eniware successful."

Tim concluded, *"So, using persuasion, like position, in the long run, was pretty pointless."*

Lesson 4: Are You Persuasive?

Persuasion accomplishes immediate tasks, but if a leader has to persuade people to perform, there's a fundamental breakdown in employees' understanding of why their work is necessary and *how* their work connects to the success of the business.

We all possess the talent to make a persuasive argument, but is this the way we should be achieving focus, urgency and accountability?

In the last 15 years, the concept of involvement in decision making has been carried over to the workplace, and industrial psychologists have urged organizations to work toward more employee involvement and empowerment. Regrettably, most models taught to managers and supervisors have an attitudinal focus (getting a buy-in on decisions), not a process-based (business) focus.

Employee involvement aimed at changing attitudes to achieve an end result is actually a method of persuasion.

Employee involvement is not bad. On the contrary, it's good. It's a huge improvement over authoritarian decision making. However, changing attitudes by building consensus takes considerable, time-consuming energy. Instead of spending time *persuading* employees to do what they should be doing, consider how much easier (and more effective) it would be to have a simple process that did the "persuading" for you and kept your employees on track.

The instrument for this process is a business scorecard which immediately shows employees the status of their work relative to overall business goals, such as quality, safety, cost, productivity, people and customer service.

When employees see the scorecard, they immediately know *why* they need to perform, because they see their work's connection to the organization's goals. And when scorecards are color-coded (red for underperforming, green for on target), a quick look drives better performance.

Later, we'll talk more about business scorecards as their value to you as a leader.

Self-Assessment 4: Do You Persuade Your Team to Higher Performance?

Honestly reflect on your leadership behaviors:

1. Do you get upset when you have to "call" an employee on work not done? Do you find yourself more concerned about keeping everyone happy and being liked than in truly holding people accountable for their work?

2. Look at your to-do list, and analyze the tasks on it. Have you listed work or tasks others *could* or *should* be doing, simply because you know it would be a struggle to convince them to do it?

3. Think about the level of employee engagement on your team – how much employees buy in to their work and the goals of the department and company. Are your good intentions actually diminishing employee engagement? That is, are you perpetuating a culture of *selective* engagement based on personality – by relying on individuals you know will go the extra mile and ignoring those who refuse to do more than just get by?

4. Is your organization dependent on you to be the conduit to knowing how the organization or team is performing (winning or losing)?

Comment:

Abraham Lincoln said, "You can fool some of the people all of the time, and all of the people some of the time, but you cannot fool all of the people all of the time."

We can modify this adage a bit for our purpose: *You can please some of the people all of the time, and all of the people some of the time, But you can't please all of the people all of the time.* That's especially true for leaders. And trying to please all of your employees all of the time expends a great deal of time and energy which could be better diverted to other, more productive areas.

Instead of trying to please and persuade people to do the work they could or should be doing by appealing to "what's in it for them," hold them accountable to non-negotiable business processes – for example, full participation in team meetings and accountability to achieve team goals. Then give your employees the tools (business score-cards) they can use to keep themselves informed about their performance relative to business goals.

You'll find that you have more time, spend less (or no) energy in persuading and enjoy a higher-performing team.

Chapter 5: Performance by Proximity

Tim didn't say anything for several minutes to let his last comments soak in.

Ima mumbled his words, "Using persuasion, like position, in the long run, was pointless. Pointless ...."

Tim watched Ima out of the corner of his eye. He could see that she seemed on the verge of self-discovery, which he hoped would pull her out of her depression and regret that she was retiring. He would have to be patient. Insight into the development and progress of her leadership still eluded her, but it would come, he was sure. He wanted her to be able to leave Eniware knowing that she wasn't just turning the keys of the plant over to someone else; she was leaving a leadership legacy.

Tim turned another page of the scrapbook and pointed to another photo. It was a candid shot of a number of employees. One employee was sweeping the work area. Another seemed to be policing the aisles, picking up debris and scrap. In the foreground a worker was painting walkway lines on the floor, while another seemed to be scrubbing down a piece of equipment.

"Is this your crew, too, Ima? Wow! It looks pretty impressive. They certainly seem to be working hard that day."

Ima looked at the picture and replied, "No, they weren't my crew. I couldn't tell you when that picture was taken but I can guess the circumstances: They were probably getting ready for a VIP visit. Every time someone from headquarters made a plant visit, out came the paint brushes and the mops. You know ... everything had to look like it was kept in tip-top shape."

"But it wasn't?"

"Not really," said Ima. "When I was complaining to you about Monk and my crew a few minutes ago, it probably sounded like I was the only one who had that problem. I wasn't. Monk made my job challenging, but other supervisors were in the same boat. Getting workers to do more than 'just their job' was tough. Production standards usually were met, but other things would just be left undone, like sweeping floors, emptying trash bins, repainting lines, and washing down equipment.

"But when the president or CEO came for a visit, everybody wanted to look like they were working hard. And they did - while the execs were here. A sign of that was a clean production area. I think everyone - from the plant manager on down - was afraid that they'd get fired if the place didn't look like it was up to snuff. Everyone got a little busier than usual."

"So, if I am hearing you right, this 'looking good' and 'working hard' only happened when a manager was around. Employees worked when you or another manager was visible, but when you weren't, they let things slide."

"Well, that may be overstating it a bit. I mean ... everyone always did the core work. But the activity level always increased when the boss paid a visit - regardless of whose boss it was. If a supervisor was around, workers got busier. But once a supervisor left the area, they slacked off.

"Hmm ... It just occurred to me," she added, "maybe the workers weren't so different from the managers! I mean, keeping the plant clean was their responsibility, but making sure it was kept clean was mine - and every other supervisor's - as well as the plant manager's. Yet, we all got into gear to put it to those high standards only when the

VIPs would come around!

"I see now that no one - not even management - really accepted personal responsibility for their work back then. We all required the presence of the next higher authority to move us to get it done. ... Now that I think about it, that wasn't very effective."

"No," said Tim. "When performance requires a leader's proximity, it never is."

Lesson 5: Performance by Proximity's Shortcomings

In your experience, what happens when you - or another manager or high-level official - comes into a work area? Do employees consciously or unconsciously work harder or more diligently? Do you notice small talk diminishing and activity increasing?

It's natural for people to want to please the boss. So, in most organizations, when the leader comes around, people tend to work harder. Human nature dictates that they want to look good, even if their "work" is an act.

Proximity is directly linked to confidence. Leaders who feel connected, who are "tied in" to the workforce often use proximity as a catalyst. That is: When they are close to their employees, their confidence is high and they exert a strong degree of focus, urgency, and accountability.

But, when they are removed from the workplace (because of traveling, training, or vacation, for example), their confidence diminishes in relation to the distance.

Some leaders relish the experience of seeing work activity speed up when they are near their employees. It gives their egos a boost. They claim that their frequent visits to work areas is part of "managing by walking around" (MBWA), and they justify their actions by pointing to the higher productivity that results from their presence.

MBWA in itself is good; it allows you see what needs to be done firsthand, and it helps connect you with the workforce.

But, if you rely on MBWA to get improved performance from your employees and it is your only way of knowing what people are doing, then you are leading by proximity - one of the phenomena of managing by personality. In other words, the sheer power of your personality influences employees to perform to a higher degree. Their performance is not connected to business necessity, nor do they perform out of a sense of accountability for what needs to be done to make the organization successful.

Performance by proximity is short-termed and is sustained only as long as you are with the organization. Performance resulting from accountability and a focus on goal achievement, on the other hand, are long-lasting. They are a legacy of your leadership.

Self-Assessment 5: Proximity Assessment

1. Do you manage by walking around? What is your goal when you MBWA? What would your employees say you do?

2. How much time do you spend with your team? Do you feel you should spend more time with them? Why?

3. When you are out of the area (such as when you travel, participate in training sessions, or attend conferences), do you find yourself anxious about what is happening in the workplace? Do you make frequent calls to find out the status of things and to make sure you are available to solve problems?

4. Do you sense a heightened level of urgency among employees when you are walking through the area?

5. When you conduct performance appraisals, do you struggle to find relevant, fact-based performance data, because, in essence, the only performance data you have is from your own personal accounts?

6. Do you have 100 percent confidence that the same levels of focus, urgency, and accountability are present when you are not in the work area as when you are?

Comment:

Examine your answers to these questions. If you find that you rely on the strength of your physical presence to be assured that work is getting done to your expectations, you are leading by proximity. It's time to regroup and put into place processes that will provide your team with a sense of urgency, focus, and accountability.

Chapter 6: Personality Flaws

Ima's comments about accountability led Tim to think that maybe she was on the verge of discovering the legacy she was leaving. Accountability, after all, was a keystone of great leadership. Great leaders engendered it, and they lived by it. It was the opposite of managing by personality.

Ima, like virtually all of the supervisors at Eniware, had been "guilty" of managing by personality instead of managing with a business focus. They used the force of their personalities to get things done. And they also put their management efforts into relying on responsible workers, letting the others just "get by" in doing their work. That was the essence of managing by personality.

Fortunately for Ima and for Eniware, she had changed her ways when she climbed out of her management dumpster. She had learned to manage with a business focus – using visible and auditable systems of accountability and communication to achieve the company's business goals as the cornerstones of leading the workforce. *That was the beginning of a new era, one that has sustained itself,* thought Tim. *And it will continue to endure. Unfortunately, Ima doesn't see that.*

Tim thought that if they looked through the entire scrapbook, she would see how her leadership had changed. He turned another page and was about to say something when Ima abruptly stood up.

"Hey, where are you going? We still have a few more years of memories to catch up on!"

Ima reached over to the scrapbook and closed its pages. "I've seen enough. These pictures struck a raw nerve. They reminded me how it was back then. I relied on my personality and played on the personalities of my employees to get work done."

"What do you mean?" asked Tim, still hoping that Ima had "gotten" it.

"It's just like you were saying. I used position, persuasion, and proximity to get work accomplished. Sometimes I used them all at the same time!" she exclaimed.

"I got my crew to do things 'because I said so.' And when that didn't work, I cajoled them by appealing to their baser needs. And all the while, I hovered over them like a hawk, watching to make sure they did what I wanted. And when that didn't work, I did it myself!"

Tim had been certain that Ima's insights would lead her to see that what she was describing had been true *then; now* was a different story. She was a great leader who would leave her mark behind.

But he was disappointed.

Ima picked up her jacket and purse and walked toward the door.

"It's a good thing the new guy is coming in tomorrow," said Ima. "It's definitely time for me to leave. I just hope he does a better job of managing this plant than I did."

With that, she said, "Would you do me a favor and lock the door on the way out? I'll see you in the morning."

Tim was dumbfounded. The trip down memory lane had failed. Instead of realizing how much she'd grown as a leader and what a good job she had done, Ima had become even more depressed. She was convinced that nothing she'd done was worthwhile.

Tim watched her walk slowly and dejectedly down the hallway. He shook his head and thought, *Ima, why can't you see your leadership legacy?*

Lesson 6: The Lost Cause of Managing by Personality

Make no mistake: Most leaders today put in long hours and work very hard. They have more on their plates today than ever before.

These leaders are well trained on the tenets of effective leadership. They have at their fingertips information on implementing best practices and procedures. Yet, despite all these resources, many leaders feel overwhelmed and ineffective.

Why is this?

The answer is simple: They have been trained and conditioned to manage by personality. This conditioning is exhibited in three distinct ways:

- Managing by position,
- Managing by persuasion, and
- Managing by proximity.

It is true that managing by these three methods gets results. Many organizations have been driven to successful heights by leaders who practiced and institutionalized managing by personality. But the question begs: How do these management methods fit into a leadership legacy?

The answer: They *don't* fit; they are incompatible with legacy leadership.

Each of the three ways of managing by personality relies on a single factor – the individual leader. Remove the individual leader from the performance equation, and you remove the catalyst that drives performance; the team flounders and fails.

True, you create your own leadership legacy. But a legacy that lives on after you leave is one that is sustained by processes – processes that are *not* dependent on you to administer, maintain, or drive them.

A leadership legacy formed on processes gives your employees three vital elements:

- Clarity of communication – having confidence that people are informed and engaged;
- Connectivity to the business – focusing people on what they have in common, not what they have in conflict, and letting them know if we are winning or losing; and
- Consistency – using a visible and auditable operating system to manage the business.

Self-Assessment 6: Do You Manage by Personality

1. Do you find yourself working harder than ever before, but not accomplishing as much as you think you should?

2. Does your team rely solely on you to give them direction?

3. What happens when you're on vacation, at a seminar or sick? Are you confident that your team is performing at its highest performance levels without your presence?

4. Do you rely on certain individuals to get things done?

5. Do you find yourself saying (or implying) "because I said so" to drive performance?

6. Do you find yourself bargaining with employees to get them to perform?

7. Does life as a leader seem to be one constant negotiation?

Comment:

If you find yourself guilty of managing by position, persuasion, and/or proximity to take your team's performance to the next higher level, it's time to regroup and replace the 3 Ps with the 3 Cs: clarity, connectivity, and consistency.

A Final Thought on the 3 Ps

To this point, we (and Ima) have focused on leadership tactics that detract from leaving a legacy – proximity, persuasion and position. Although many leaders have been effective in taking their organizations to new heights using the 3 Ps, the results they achieve are at best temporary.

Now it's time for us (and Ima) to regroup and refocus. If the 3 Ps are not the answer to leaving a legacy, what is? The 3 C's: clarity, consistency and connectivity. Leaders who manage their organizations with processes that exhibit clarity, consistency and connectivity accomplish results that outlive them. They leave a leadership legacy.

Chapter 7: The New Man

Neuman Lerner pulled into the employee parking lot at the Eniware plant and found a parking space.

He turned the ignition off and sat in the car for a moment before opening the door. *Well, this is it,* he said to himself. *My first day as plant manager!*

Neuman was nervous. This was a big promotion for him. He had worked for the company for several years, holding increasingly responsible positions in production, logistics and quality control. Advancing any more meant taking on the responsibility of an entire plant. But was he really ready for this? He wasn't sure, though the company president had been.

He thought back to when the president had asked him if he would be interested in managing the Eniware plant. At first he was elated. Then he felt both gratified and scared. Eniware had a great reputation, so to be given the responsibility of plant manager was an honor. And he didn't want to screw it up.

Neuman did not accept the job on the spot. Instead, he did some homework, because he wanted to know what he would be walking into. He wanted to make sure it was something he could handle.

It amounted to knowing yourself, he had thought. I know what my strengths are – and my weaknesses. I'm not afraid to own up to them. I can continue to make a good plant shine, but if Eniware requires a major turnaround, then it would be better to leave that task to someone with the talent and skills to handle it. I know I can make incremental changes, but if there are big problems …

Neuman's homework, though, seemed to indicate that the Eniware plant was going to be a great match for him. The current plant manager, Ima Manijer, had done a impressive job. She was the one who had turned the plant around. Somehow (he didn't know how) she had taken the plant from one with a fair reputation for meeting goals to one whose name was synonymous with great customer service, extraordinary quality and superior production achievement. The plant had consistently set records for fewest customer complaints, lowest down time, highest quality, highest employee satisfaction, best safety records and most on-time deliveries. *It would be quite a reputation to uphold,* he thought.

Neuman was in awe of Ima Manijer. *How had she been able to accomplish so much?* he asked himself. Although he would spend just a short time with her before she retired, he intended to try to find out.

So here he was, sitting in his car, first day on the job, and a nervous wreck. He finally opened the door, got out of the car, retrieved his brief case and walked toward the administration building.

Chapter 8: A Clear Direction

Neuman walked down the hallway of the administration building until he found the office marked "Plant Manager." He knocked and entered. No one was there.

That's odd, he thought. *I wonder where everyone is? I know they are expecting me.*

He was going to sit down to wait when he heard some laughter from what appeared to be a small conference room just off the waiting area of the plant manager's office. The door was slightly ajar. Curious, he pulled it open a few inches more and peeked inside, where he saw a group of men and women sitting around a conference table. At the head of the table, near a flip chart, was a woman whom Neuman guessed was Ima Manijer.

As he was peering into the room, Tim Leder, who was sitting next to Ima, looked up and saw him. "Hi, Neuman. Come on in. ... Everyone, this is Neuman Lerner, your new plant manager."

Neuman opened the door and entered the room. "I didn't realize there was a meeting this morning," he apologized, slightly red in the face.

"Welcome," smiled Ima cordially. "Please! Don't worry ... Your timing couldn't be better, because, as you can see," she pointed to the meeting agenda, "the next topic we were going to discuss was *you!*"

A few minutes later, with all introductions complete, the meeting broke up, and the team members went back to their own departments. Ima, Tim, and Neuman stayed behind in the conference room.

"Was there a particular reason for the meeting this morning, Ima? Anything I should know about?" Neuman asked.

"Nothing special," replied Ima. "We meet every week to make sure everyone is up to date - myself included. This is when everyone finds out the overall status of the operations in each of several areas - production, quality, customer service, safety, cost, and people. And if there is a problem, we make note of it and plan on how it should be fixed. And it's a time when I can pass down information to employees."

She pointed to the wall where an electronic projection was visible. On it was a type of grid; it looked like some type of planning form, but a big one that was easily read even from the back of the room.

"This is our plant scorecard," explained Ima. "We monitor our plant goals. And we update it weekly. We use a color code to signal our progress."

"Hey, that's pretty ingenious," said Neuman. "I mean ... I've used a scorecard with graphs and charts to show project status for a long time, but this is different. It reminds me of those 'thermometers' they use in United Way drives. I mean, it's not a thermometer, but it works the same way, doesn't it? I can see at a glance how the plant is doing because of the color coding. I can easily guess that green means 'everything's OK' and red means 'we have a problem.' By the looks of this chart with all of its green, the plant is really doing well!"

Ima tilted her head as if she were looking at the scorecard for the first time. "Hmm ... I've gotten so used to using this scorecard - it's a way of life here - that I hadn't thought of it in those terms. But, yes, it is a kind of thermometer."

Tim hoped that Neuman's recognition of the scorecard

might cause Ima to start thinking in terms of what she was leaving behind. But if it did, she gave no indication. Instead, she said, "Well! Let's get you settled in and then take a tour of the plant. I know you are probably eager to get to work!"

As Ima brushed off the importance of the scorecard - one of the pieces of the legacy she was leaving behind - Tim thought: *She's putting up a good front today, but deep down, nothing has changed. She's still feeling bad about leaving the plant, even though she is doing a great job of making her replacement feel at home. She doesn't realize how much of her will live on. I hope we can make her see it so that she will feel good about handing over the keys to the plant to Neuman Lerner.*

+++

After showing Neuman his office and getting him a hard hat, safety glasses, and safety shoes, Ima and Tim were ready to take him on a plant tour.

"Oh, wait just a moment!" he said. He rummaged in his brief case and took out a clipboard and pen. "OK. Now I'm ready. I want to take a lot of notes."

As they walked toward their first stop, the production floor, Neuman saw a small group of employees exiting a room marked "team leader's office," while another group got ready to go in.

"What's going on over there?" he asked.

"A scorecard meeting," answered Ima.

"A scorecard meeting? Is it something like your weekly team meeting?"

"Yes," answered Ima. "Everyone here at Eniware belongs to a home team — my department managers belong to my primary team; each of the supervisors belongs to the team of a department manager. And all employees who form a natural work team belong to their supervisor's team. Come on ... let's go sit in for a few minutes. It'll be a good way to meet a few employees and see how the scorecard meetings work."

The three managers sat in the back of the room. The team leader was preparing the room as his group gathered around the table. Ima made the introductions, and the meeting started.

As the team meeting began, Neuman looked around the conference room. The first thing he noticed was a flip chart with an agenda posted on it. The agenda had on it most of the items that had been listed on the agenda he had seen in Ima's meeting.

Then he saw the scorecard. It was almost - but not quite - identical to the one in Ima's conference room. It used the same format and colors, and listed the same focus areas: production, quality, customer service, safety, cost, and people. And, just like the one in Ima's office, it was projected onto the wall through a computer hooked up to the projector.

When the meeting was adjourned - on time, according to the agenda, which had time limits placed on each agenda item - Neuman walked over to the agenda and the scorecard.

"This agenda. It seems to include the items that you covered in your meeting."

"Yes, that's true. Obviously, I can't be everywhere, but I want to make sure that the same messages are delivered to all employees. One way we do that is to make sure we cascade information downward. And *upward,* I might add.

"Upward?"

"Yes. Information about accomplishments - and problems - are sent upward through the home-team meetings, so we all are aware of them and can act on them appropriately - like saying thank-you for a great job or intervening with some help when its needed. We talk about these things."

Neuman said, "Where I come from, we used bulletin boards to keep people informed. We'd post good news, like beating production or quality goals or acknowledging individual accomplishments. We also had electronic message boards we used quite a bit - especially to remind people to work safely."

Ima hesitated before she commented. "Were the exact same messages posted in every department?"

"Good point. No, not always."

"And did everyone read the bulletin board?"

"Well, I can't say so, for sure. You know how people are."

"Yes, people don't always read everything you give them. That's one reason we have the team meetings - to make sure everyone gets the same message at the same time. Another thing is this: *What you talk about is what is important.* And, like it or not, what the plant manager talks about is *really* important! So, when the agenda cascades down from the top and the same things are covered as in the plant manager's home team, people know that it's important. Finally, the team meetings let us *really* communicate - face to face. Because, let's face it - a bulletin board or electronic sign can't talk or listen. They do a good job of advertising, though! In a team meeting, both talking and listening happen. "

Neuman scribbled notes as fast as he could. Then he asked, "That chart that's projected on the wall - the business scorecard - it looks very similar to the one you had posted in your meeting this morning."

"Yes, but this one is for this team."

"Does every team use one of these?

Ima looked at the scorecard and said matter of factly, "Yes, of course. It keeps everyone on course. Everyone has a clear understanding of what is expected of them."

"In some places where I've worked," reflected Neuman, "the plant manager and his immediate managers always knew the status of the plant. But employees rarely did. In other places, we shared information about the status of work through charts similar to this one."

Neuman peered silently at the scorecard for a few minutes. Then his face lit up. "I see what's different now! It's staring me right in the face, it's so obvious! Your scorecard and the scorecard for this team use the same *business terms* - production, quality, customer service, safety, cost, and people! Everyone is held accountable for the *same* things, so anyone walking into this team's meeting can immediately understand what's going on.

"This is really a neat idea! Your system aligns all the goals throughout the plant. *Everyone* knows at a glance how the plant is doing - and what they need to do to reach a goal."

"That's the idea," said Ima. "We've done it so long here, we don't think twice about it. We also use this" - she clicked the mouse of the computer - "an action register." The projected image listed actions that the team needed to do to accomplish its various goals. Each action item was followed by the name of the individual responsible to make sure it was done, a timetable for accomplishing the action, and a place to indicate if (and when) the action was completed.

"The action register is important," continued Ima, "because it assigns accountability to get things done. We all use it - everywhere in the plant."

"That's ingenious," mumbled Neuman. "I've got to write this down." He began taking notes and spoke out loud as he wrote: "Everyone belongs to a team. Each team meets weekly. Every team uses an agenda to assure that the right information is flowing downward and upward. What is talked about is important, so the team meeting permits face-to-face communication. And every team uses a business scorecard that uses the same language. The scorecard sets performance expectations and an action register assigns accountability to every team member."

He looked up at Ima and Tim. "Does that about sum it up?"

Tim deferred to Ima, who looked thoughtful for a moment. "Yes. That's a good summary of what you've observed."

Neuman said, "Ima, this is a good system you've put into place. I've read time and again that the No. 1 universal employee complaint is 'lack of communication.' Managers are always perplexed by that complaint, because they put out bulletins and memos, and they tell employees what to do - like produce x-number of widgets a day. But those same managers invariably fail to relate their employees' jobs with the overall goals of the plant."

Neuman looked thoughtful for a moment, then continued. "A few years ago I took a tour of an electrical-components manufacturing plant. The parts the plant made were used in the automotive industry. The tour group stopped to watch workers engaged in soldering small parts. I asked a woman, 'What's that part used in?' She looked up from her work and answered, 'I don't really know.'

"Two of that plant's biggest problems were low productivity and poor quality. It's a sure bet those employees did not have any type of scorecard, team meeting, or action register that kept them focused on the bigger picture.

"What you've done here is to put into place a clear-cut process that ensures clarity - of purpose, expectations, and performance. And because these things are tied back to the plant's goals, people understand why they need to do their best. It's like those nesting toys you give to babies - the little egg fits into a bigger egg, which fits into a bigger egg, etc. My hat is off to you."

Ima's cheeks reddened as Neuman finished his short discourse. "Thank you, Neuman. I appreciate hearing that." Then, under her breath, she repeated Neuman's words, *"A clear-cut process that ensures clarity."*

Tim overheard her whisper and smiled. *I think she might be getting it,* he thought.

Lesson 8: Clarity as a Characteristic of Legacy Leadership

Clarity is essential in creating a leadership legacy, and clarity is only achieved through a defined process of communication.

Leadership brings with it the obligation to create and sustain a robust communication process that drives focus, urgency, and accountability. That communication process must be ongoing and renewed regularly - usually weekly. And the communication process must not be dependent on the leader's proximity, persuasion, or position. Instead, it must be built on repeatable non-negotiable processes.

To drive this clarity, certain elements must be in place:
• A non-negotiable agenda to use in all team meetings,
  • A business scorecard,
  • An action register system, and
  • A pass-down/pass-up process of communication.

Non-negotiable agenda

In process-based leadership, certain minimum standards (non-negotiables) affect everyone - from the top manager on down the line. One of these non-negotiables is that everyone belongs to and participates in a team. And when the team meets, it maintains its order through a non-negotiable agenda, the first element that ensures clear communication in an organization.

The agenda sets the stage for focused communication in the team meetings. It also drives urgency throughout the organization.

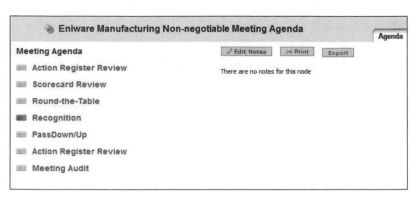

All agendas include the same items:

1. Action register review. This is a review of the team's action register — items that are scheduled to be completed.

2. Scorecard review. This is a review of the team's business scorecard, with discussion about corrective actions for red scorecard performances;

3. Around the table discussion. The team engages in an around-the-table discussion of problems, concerns, and contingencies.

4. Recognition. With the agenda item, team members recognize achievements (team and individual) made since the last team meeting.

5. Pass up/pass down. This is a sharing of information that everyone needs to be aware of - information that needs to be passed up throughout the organization as well as information that needs to be passed down the organization, to assure everyone is in the know.

6. Review of the action register. The team goes over the action register to make sure that everyone understands his or her next steps and assignments.

7. An audit of the meeting. The team goes over what

went well, what did not go well in the meeting and how could the meeting be improved.

Because each team uses the same agenda, all information is clearly communicated throughout the organization.

Business Scorecard

The next element that drives clarity is a business scorecard.

As a leader, one of your chief responsibilities is to instill a singular business focus within the workplace - to put into place a process that communicates the business need for top performance.

A tool that allows this to happen is the business scorecard - a system the team uses to list goals and track them easily through color coding. (Goals that are on target of being met are coded green; those that fall below expectations are coded red.) This system ensures a direct link between the overall company or facility goals and departmental objectives as they cascade throughout the organization.

The scorecard is effective, because it becomes the organization's common business language.

However, for the scorecard to become the organization's common business language, it must:

1. Identify key focus areas. The key focus areas should be derived from the organizational vision or mission statement. These areas are themes or categories that *all* home teams must support. Key focus areas are the non-negotiable alignment component of the scorecard.

2. Use a standard format. Although each team develops goals specific to its needs and function, all teams must use the same standard scorecard format. The universal format, as well as the key focus areas, speak to the scorecard's

Eniware Manufacturing Global

Eniware Manufacturing Global

ID	Objective	Target	Responsibility	Frequency For Review	January 2007	February 2007	March 2007	April 2007	May 2007	June 2007
Safety										
2291	10% reduction in Lost Time Accidents over 2006 performance (10 LTA's in 2006) **10% reduction in Lost Time Accidents over 2007 performance**	8		Monthly						
2290	All home teams conduct month end Safety Briefing provided by Corp. Safety Council **Month end Safety Briefing**	1		Monthly						
Quality										
2289	Achieve an On Time/In Full (OTIF) rating of 98.5% **Achieve an On Time/In Full (OTIF) rating of 98.5%**	0.985%		Monthly						
2288	Maintain acceptable Scrap Levels at 2.8% or less **Maintain acceptable Scrap Levels at 2.8% or less**	2.8%		Monthly						
Cost										
2287	Maintain an overall site budget variance of +/- 3% on a monthly basis **Maintain an overall site budget variance of +/- 3% on a monthly basis**	-0.03		Monthly						
2286	Maintain an Eniware Component profitability ratio of 3.8% per unit **Maintain profitability ratio of 3.8% per unit**	3.8%		Monthly						
People										
2285	Maintain absenteeism at 3.0% or less **Maintain absenteeism at 3.0% or less**	3%		Monthly						
2284	Reduce turnover from 11.8% to 8.0% **Reduce turnover from 11.8% to 8.0%**	8%		Monthly						
2283	Each salaried employee to find/attend one continuing education training event per year **continuing education training event per year**	2		Annual						
Customer Service										
2282	Reduce Customer Complaints by 50% over 2006 performance **Reduce Customer Complaints by 50%**	1.5		Monthly						
2281	Conduct a Monthly Customer Satisfaction Survey with a aggregate rating of 4.5 or greater in terms of Satisfaction Index **Monthly customer Satisfaction Survey**	4.5		Monthly						
Productivity										
2280	Produce 11,500 Eniware Manufacturing components per month **Eniware Manufacturing components per month**	11,500		Monthly						

69

Business Scorecard for One Key Focus Area — Cost										
Key Focus Area	Smart Objectives	target	owner	Tracking frequency visible indicator*						Comments
				Jan	Feb	Mar	Apr	May	Jun	
Cost	Reduce scrap from current 1% by end of 1st quarter.	1% or less	Amy	1.7% ☹	0.8% ☺					

"ability" to educate the workforce.

A scorecard with a standard format may have the following items:

• **A list of the key focus areas:** These are quality, safety, cost, productivity, people, and customer service.

• **SMART objectives:** SMART stands for Specific, Measurable, Achievable, Relevant, and Timely. Each team must write at least one objective for each of the key focus areas.

For example: Achieve a scrap level of 1% by end of the first quarter.

• **Target:** This is a performance target for the team. It identifies the color-coded thresholds of performance.

For example: Scrap reduction equal to or less 1%: green. Above 1%: red.

• **Owner:** The owner of the objective is not the person responsible for accomplishing it. Rather, it is the individual who is responsible for tracking the objective and updating the scorecard prior to each meeting.

• **Tracking frequency visible indicator:** The owner of the objective tracks the objective with a metric, as well as with a color - green for on target, red for failure to meet the target.

For example: Jan. (scrap level) 1.7%; Feb. 0.8%.

In our example, January would be marked red, because

it was above the objective of 1%. But February would be colored green, because the scrap level was at or below 1%.

Using a color allows each team member to diagnose the status of the team with regard to meeting its objectives. And the colors help set the tone for the meeting. If the scorecard bears a lot of red, for example, the team will focus on corrective action.

• **Comments:** The team can make comments about circumstances affecting objective achievement.

The scorecard drives continuous improvement within the team and the organization because it funnels the energy and talent of all employees in a unified direction.

3. Be updated and projected prior to the business meeting. Before the business meeting starts, each scorecard must be populated with updated information. And it must be projected for everyone to see it. This can be done electronically through a computer program or an overhead projector or posted on a flip chart.

The scorecard helps overcome a problem in today's organizations, which are overbooked with ineffective meetings that fail to have purpose or advance the business. A populated and projected scorecard sets the tone for the meeting even before a word is spoken. It demonstrates the value of the meeting. And it stops the leader from allowing the 3 P's to influence the team.

A robust scorecard process not only tells the team how it is performing, but it facilitates focus, urgency, and accountability.

4. Motivate continuous improvement. Color-coding of the scorecard enables team members to understand within seconds of looking at it, the tone of the meeting and what needs to be discussed.

Eniware Manufacturing Global

New Action | Add to Home | Print | Export

ID	Action	Applies To	Responsibility	Target Date	Completion Date	Comments	Administration
482	Maintain absenteeism at 3.0% or less -Target 3.0% or less	Eniware Manufacturing Global	Boggan, Debra	March 6, 2007 Add to Calendar		Comments	Edit History
479	Achieve an On Time/In Full (OTIF) rating of 98.5% - Target 98.5% and Greater	Eniware Manufacturing Global	Pyecha, John	March 8, 2007 Add to Calendar		Comments	Edit History
478	Maintain acceptable Scrap Levels at 2.8% or less - Target 2.8% or less	Eniware Manufacturing Global	Boggan, Debra	March 12, 2007 Add to Calendar		Comments	Edit History
481	Reduce Customer Complaints by 50% over 2006 performance -Target (36 Significant Product Complaints in 2006) - 2007 Target - 18 Product Complaints - 1.5 per month	Eniware Manufacturing Global	VerSteeg, Anna	March 13, 2007 Add to Calendar		Comments	Edit History
480	Produce 11,500 Eniware Manufacturing components per month Target 11,500 or greater	Eniware Manufacturing Global	Yount, Shane	March 19, 2007 Add to Calendar		Comments	Edit History
484	All home teams conduct month end Safety Briefing provided by Corp. Safety Council - Target- monthly	Eniware Manufacturing Global	VerSteeg, Anna	March 27, 2007 Add to Calendar		Comments	Edit History
483	Conduct a Monthly Customer Satisfaction Survey with a aggregate rating of 4.5 or greater in terms of Satisfaction Index -Target 4.5% or greater	Eniware Manufacturing Global	Yount, Shane	March 7, 2007	March 8, 2007	Comments	Archive Edit History
485	Maintain an overall site budget variance of +/- 3% on a monthly basis -Target +/- 3%	Eniware Manufacturing Global	Pyecha, John	March 9, 2007	March 12, 2007	Comments	Archive Edit History

Green items denote recognition and red items show a need for corrective action planning (action register items).

Action register: Bringing Visibility to Accountability

The third element that must be in place to assure clarity is an action register.

The action register is the logical extension of the business scorecard. The business scorecard ensures that employees focus on issues important to the success of the company.

But focus is not performance. Performance is achieved when people are held accountable to act on the objectives that support the business.

The action register is the tool that drives accountability throughout the organization. It publicly documents the assignment of tasks to specific individuals, dates for completion of tasks, and results.

The example on the top of the page that follows demonstrates how the action register works.

When leaders implement the use of this tool along with the business scorecard, they eliminate ignorance as an excuse for tasks not completed, and they eliminate personality from the focus of business.

And they can see at a glance the level of engagement of their team members. All team members are assigned tasks to complete. Those who are on target for completion are fully engaged.

Action registers are created as part of the process to achieve goals identified on the business scorecard. They serve as an archive of accomplishment, a gauge of productivity, a mechanism to record correction-action plans, and a method to manage performance.

Action Register				
Objective: Beginning Jan. 1, reduce scrap from current 3% level to 1% by end of 1st quarter				
ACTION	**RESPONSIBILITY**	**TARGET**	**COMPLETED**	**COMMENTS**
Verify equipment specifications and calibration with maintenance	Harvey	January 5	January 5	Completed. Califbration set to standard.
Assess technical training needs for team members	Mary	January 15		Assessment tool completed and passed out January 7. Will compile results and report to team by target
Identify cause of scrap	Jim	January 15	January 15	Long changeover time is resulting in scrap.
Vendor certification — is raw material from suppliers meeting specifications?	Cathy	January 5	January 5	Raw material meets specs

Pass-down/pass-up communication

The fourth element to ensure clarity is pass-down / pass-up communication.

Communication, by definition, is a two-way process. Although leaders cannot be everywhere and personally be able to get and give information to every single individual in the organization, they can put into place a process that ensures two-way communication.

Through Home Team Meetings held regularly (usually weekly), leaders share information on the status of business, the problems the company faces, and the successes the company enjoys. This is pass-down information that each team leader takes to his or her team and shares.

And in these meetings, information about problems encountered at lower levels as well as the success of individuals and teams is communicated upward and laterally throughout the organization in meetings in which team members can ask questions and get clarity. This is pass-up information, which is important for higher-level leaders to know of problems and successes so they can act appropriately on the information.

The Eniware Manufacturing Benefits Package is changing
Passed down from Eniware Manufacturing Non-negotiable Meeting Agenda on 3/9/2007 at 1:23 PM

The Eniware Manufacturing Benefits Package is changing. Critical new components are as follows:

- We are transitioning from Red Flag Healthcare to Green Light Medical Providers
- Family deductibles will be going from $100 to $250
- Co-pays will be going from $10 to $20 per visit
- Both dental and vision coverages will remain unchanged
- Please register with Donna in HR your latest dependent information by September 1st

pass to | delete

Please welcome our new Plant Manager
Passed down from Eniware Manufacturing Non-negotiable Meeting Agenda on 3/12/2007 at 9:34 AM

Please welcome our new Plant Manager, Newman Lerner. Mr. Lerner comes to us from leading our global supply chain organization at our sister facility. Mr. Lerner will touring the facility on Friday with our North American Vice President, Tim Leder and our current Plant Manager, Ima Manijer. Please make him feel welcome as we transition our new leader into Eniware Manufacturing

pass to | delete

Self-Assessment 8: Do You Give a Clear Direction?

1. Do employees use ignorance as an excuse for not accepting accountability? That is, do you hear excuses such as "I didn't know that was what you wanted" or "I wasn't trained on that"?

2. Do employees get most of their information through the rumor mill?

3. If you were to walk out among your employees right now and randomly ask any of them to recite the company's business goals, would they be able to do it?

4. Are you confident your employees know the status of the company? How do they become privy to that information?

5. How do you communicate the status of goal achievement?

6. How do you communicate successes?

7. How do you learn about the successes and problems that occur in lower levels of the organization?

8. How do you ensure that key information is communicated to everyone within your organization?

9. Do you have regular meetings with your immediate team? Do your team members meet with their employees following your meeting?

10. How are employees held accountable for performance?

11. How do you manage consistent employee engagement?

Comment:

The top complaint of employees in every organization (large or small) is lack of communication. Managers always believe they communicate well; employees know differently.

Communication, by definition, is a two-way process of providing and receiving information. When two people communicate face-to-face, one sends a message; the other acknowledges it and in that acknowledgement, gives feedback; and the first responds to the feedback. The process continues until understanding is achieved.

The typical ways in which organizations "communicate" - through bulletin boards, e-mails, memos, electronic signs, and newsletters - fall short of true communication. These methods are one-sided, because they do not allow for feedback, clarification, and subsequent understanding. At their best, these passive means of "communication" advertise what needs to be communicated.

The only way to ensure communication is to put into place a regular non-negotiable communication process - one that reinforces what is important.

Communication is the core of a good leadership legacy.

Chapter 9: By the Book

Tim, Ima, and Neuman continued on their plant tour. They walked up and down the production floor. Ima pointed out the various working groups and explained the work the teams were engaged in.

They stopped to watch two workers. One seemed to be teaching the other how to do a procedure. Ima explained what was occurring: "George is training Sheila to run this machine. Because quality control is important to customer satisfaction, right now he's showing her how to take a sample, measure its quality, note it on a chart and adjust the machine if the quality chart shows that an adjustment is needed."

"Is he the team's trainer? I mean, usually that job is reserved for a very senior person who's been doing the job for a long time. But George looks pretty young."

Ima replied, "We don't have team trainers as such. Once people master a process, they can then train others."

"How do you know it's done right?" asked Neuman.

"That's easy ... they use the team handbook to guide them," said Ima.

Neuman started to ask, "What's a team hand..." but before he could finish his question, a team leader who looked upset came over to talk with Ima. After she made introductions, he said, "Ima, I've got a problem. Frank was late getting back from his break again this morning. We have to do something about this because it's affecting everyone else's work."

Ima asked, "What does your team handbook say about this type of problem?"

"It says I should confront him," he says. "I've already done that, and he's continued coming in late."

"So what's the next step?" asked Ima.

The team leader thought for a moment. "I guess the next step is to take it to the team. The team established the consequences for tardiness. He was even part of that discussion."

Ima smiled, "Then you know what you have to do." The team leader nodded and went back to his work group.

Neuman looked at Ima, a bit in awe of her. "*That* was something else! I guess my first impulse would have been to solve the problem myself ... to tell that team leader to send Frank to my office."

Ima laughed. "Yes, a few years ago, that's what I would have done, too! But then, the tardiness would have become my problem! And I have enough problems to deal with! It's really a team problem, and the team leader just needed to be reminded that the solution to the problem was already spelled out in his team handbook."

"That's the second time in only a few minutes you have referred to the 'team handbook.' What is it?"

"It's probably easier to show you than to tell you. Let's go take a look at one," said Ima. They turned back toward the team leader's office, where they found a copy of the handbook. Neuman leafed through it.

Ima explained the concept of the book as he turned the pages. "The team handbook is kind of an SOP – you know, standing operating procedure – for the team," she said. "In it you'll find the team's action registers, communication processes and behavior expectations."

"So this document," said Neuman, taking notes, "spells out accountability for work performance to achieve overall goals. It gives detailed descriptions of the work that needs to be done. Hmmm … and I see that those descriptions are written so that the trainers can use them to make sure everyone does the job in the same, consistent way. And in addition to all of that, the handbook sets out expectations for behavior, such as attendance, tardiness and participation in team meetings, and what's to be done when the team rules are broken."

"That's right," said Ima.

"This is really ingenious. How did you come up with it?"

"Well, it took a while," reflected Ima. "Early in my career, I worked for several different managers and supervisors. Some of them were good; others not so good. The supervisors who *weren't* very good always had a lot of personnel problems: Some people seemed to get away with coming in late, or taking long breaks, or not doing their job, and the others would resent that."

"Yeah," interjected Neuman, "I've seen that, too. Good workers get 'rewarded' by getting more work, while the poor workers get out of doing work because supervisors find it too hard to make them do it! And then the good workers get mad because everything is dumped on them! They say things aren't fair. And they're right."

"Exactly!" said Ima. "I confess that even I was guilty of that when I first started managing. But it finally dawned on me that the root cause of most of that conflict was inconsistency – in expectations and accountability. Remember: the number one reason why people get out of being held accountable is that they plead ignorance. 'I didn't know I was supposed to do that!' they claim.

"Now we don't have that problem. The team handbook

takes that excuse away. It removes ignorance as an excuse and elevates expectations of engagement by holding everyone accountable. Along with the action registers, the team handbook sets out expectations for behavior – and provides a mechanism for team leaders to be consistent."

"Clarity. Consistency. All through teams, home team meetings, action registers, and team handbooks. Ima, I'm so glad we are taking this tour this morning," said Neuman. "I can't wait to see what else you've put in place in this plant."

Ima blinked at the compliment.

Tim smiled.

Lesson 9: Consistency by the Book

Managing by personality creates an inconsistent workplace. People never know what to expect. Managing by process, on the other hand, drives consistency.

Influential and effective leaders are often characterized as being consistent. They have a strategy; they stay the course; they know how to get there. They stay constant, stable, unwavering, solid.

Consistency starts with clearly communicating expectations and consequences for failing to meet them, in behavioral language.

It is then carried out by providing non-negotiable methods to manage the business process. These methods include business scorecards, team meetings and team handbooks:

• **Business scorecards.** As we have already seen, business scorecards give consistency to the communication process because they use a common language and appearance: All teams "speak" the language of achieving goals for production, quality, customer service, safety, cost and people.

• **Team meetings.** As a non-negotiable process, all team members belong to and participate on a team, which meets regularly (usually weekly). All team meetings use a consistent agenda that includes a review of scorecards, discussion of problem areas, and pass-up and pass-down information. Using the same agenda assures consistent information flow.

• **Team handbook.** A third method of achieving consistency is to "rule" by the book – the team handbook, that is.

A handbook is a document prepared by the team. It:

√ Gives order to meetings by spelling out the agenda.

√ Gives a business focus to work by documenting the business scorecard and action registers.

√ Outlines procedures for work done in the department.

√ Serves as a history of performance (through the action registers).

√ Is a public record, accessible to all team members.

Scorecards, team meetings, and the team handbook are the foundations for consistent communication in your leadership legacy.

Self-Assessment 9: Are You Consistent?

1. Are your expectations clearly defined and written down?

2. Do your employees plead "I didn't know I was supposed to do that" when they fail to meet your expectations?

3. If you were to leave your current position, what type of orientation process would you have in place to acclimate the new leader to the team and its processes?

4. Does your organization have an expectation for new leaders to "make the team their own" – that is, to "reinvent" team leadership, complete with new expectations and rules of engagement?

5. Do leaders within the same department or division have different operation systems that make their individual organizations feel like separate companies?

Comment:

An unhappy workforce is an unproductive workforce. And a chief cause of an unhappy workforce is inconsistent treatment by their leaders. Instituting a system to achieve consistency is a hallmark characteristic of leaving a leadership legacy.

We as leaders have to worry less about how to motivate our people and worry more about the things we do that demotivate. Inconsistent expectations of engagement demotivate high performance. It is the leader's job to create and sustain a process that insures action visibility and equality.

Chapter 10: Connecting

The Eniware plant employed more than 500 people who worked three shifts a day, seven days a week. It consisted of shipping and receiving; a parts department, (where parts used in the assembly of final product were fabricated); an assembly department (where final product assembly was done); a quality assurance department; a maintenance department; and administrative support departments such as human resources, payroll and information technology.

Ima and Tim had taken Neuman to several of these areas, but they still had a few to go. "Why don't we continue the tour? I don't want you to get lost the first time you go out on your own," she joked.

They headed out of the production area into the maintenance department, where they watched workers rebuilding and repairing machine parts and equipment. As she had done in other departments, Ima introduced the new plant manager, who talked with workers and took many notes.

They started to go toward the quality assurance area, when Neuman noticed a sign pointing to the men's restroom. "Just a minute," he said sheepishly.

As he emerged from the restroom and walked back toward Ima and Tim, Neuman saw the plant's janitor, who was emptying some trash. "Excuse me," he said. "Are you the janitor who takes care of the men's room?"

The worker looked up from his task. "Yes, sir. Is there a problem?"

"Oh, no!" said Neuman. "I'm Neuman Lerner, the new

plant manager. I just wanted to tell you how impressed I am. I just came out of the men's room over there. It was really neat and clean! In fact, I've never been in a men's room in a production facility that was so clean."

"Why, thank you," said the janitor, with a hint of pride in his voice. "It's not too hard to keep it that way, because the people here tend to pick up after themselves. We're all proud of Eniware and like to keep it feeling like home. We all have a job to do, and I figure that if I do mine well enough, it helps the others do theirs better."

"How so?"

"The way I figure it is this: If people feel good about the little things, like having a clean area to wash their hands or not finding trash all over the floor, then they feel good about working here. And when people like where they work, they usually do a better job – you know, taking more care to make sure things are done right, 'cause it's theirs. So if I do my job right, then other people will do their jobs right, too. Like I said, I try to do my part."

"That's a great attitude," said Neuman genuinely. "Keep up the good work. I hope all of Eniware's employees are like you. It will make my job easy."

Neuman rejoined Tim and Ima, and they continued with the plant tour. But he couldn't stop talking about the janitor and the men's room. "I can't get over the condition of that men's room … and I was really surprised at what the janitor told me. I've never heard a janitor link his job to the quality of work done in the plant before."

Ima commented, "Since everybody – even the janitor – belongs to a home team, they 'get' the big picture. We try to link everything together so that everyone has a buy-in about how his job affects everyone else's job."

"Does that also account for how clean the plant is? Because it really is clean — not just the men's room. Or did you put out an all-points bulletin for everyone do a special cleanup today?"

Ima laughed. "No, that's just another example of how we do things around here," she said. "Tim and I were talking about that VIP phenomenon yesterday. Years ago, people got busy when a guest or vice president or other bigwig came around. Not anymore. People have their jobs to do, and they do them, right down to their least favorite tasks, like sweeping aisles, picking up trash and painting machinery. They really understand how their work affects our profitability and success and, ultimately, their jobs."

"But how do you do that? I mean … in many places, some of the workers only care about their paycheck, their vacation, and their benefits — in essence, their needs, not the company's."

"I know what you mean," answered Ima. "That's an entitlement mindset. It says, 'You owe me! I deserve it!' I think what we've managed to do here is to develop a different kind of mindset, one that says, 'We owe each other.' There's a give and take. Employees know that their jobs are important - to them, but also to the company. And the company – and by that I mean all of us in management – know and value the jobs and the people who hold them. Because without those people, the work *couldn't* get done, and the company couldn't be successful."

"Yes, I see that," said Neuman. "But *how* did you do it?"

Ima shrugged, "I guess by doing the things we've already talked about — communicating face to face in team meetings, being accountable, sending consistent messages about what is important – production, cost, quality, safety, customer service and people (but not necessarily in that order!) – being clear about what has to be done, letting people see how their jobs interact with each other and affect the company's bottom line. And by caring."

Neuman nodded and looked down at Ima's feet. "Ima … what size shoes do you wear?"

"Shoe size? Why in the world would you want to know that?" she asked, astonished.

"Because I have a feeling I am going to have trouble filling them when you leave!"

Tim saw Ima blush. All she said was, "Thank you."

Lesson 10: Connecting the People with the Business

A key to legacy leadership is connectivity. Performance is achieved when team members feel connected to the business. If they don't feel this connection, they reconnect to their individual wants and needs. This breeds and perpetuates an entitlement mentality. Leaving a leadership legacy requires a system that links people to the business and to an understanding that winning or losing in business binds them together with a common purpose. This connectivity is achieved through the use of business scorecards.

A business scorecard should be simple and concise. It should reflect and become the common business language of the organization.

Measuring performance is not a new concept by any means. But having in place a process that drives a consistent business focus is new.

As a leader, you want to put into place a robust scorecard system that:

• **Educates.** The scorecard should teach people what is important and why it is important. It should teach the value of winning and the consequences of losing.

• **Facilitates.** A vigorous scorecard is all you need to facilitate an effective team. If the scorecard is populated with the status of goal accomplishment prior to your team meeting and is visually projected during the meeting so that everyone can see it, it becomes the driving facilitative factor of the meeting.

Green items trigger recognition of accomplishments; red items trigger discussion, problem solving, and planning, all documented in the team action register with specific names and target dates for completion.

• **Motivates.** The color-coded scorecard is a visual motivator that drives the team to accomplish its goals. Without this scorecard, leadership reverts to the 3 Ps (power, persuasion, and proximity – managing by personality) to engage employees to perform.

The scorecard provides consistency and constancy. It drives the business.

Self-Assessment 10: Do Your Employees Connect with the Business?

1. In most organizations, each department has its own goals and objectives. In process-based leadership, all goals and objectives are linked together, because what happens in one department affects what happens in another. If you were to examine the goals and objectives established for all departments throughout your organization, would you find that they use a common business language? Or are the goals of each department focused only on the functioning of that department?

2. Do the different teams/departments in your organization each have their own goal-tracking process, each with a different look and format?

3. For an organization to be successful, its members must understand how strategy and tactical support systems are connected. Can you explain this? And just as important, can your employees explain it?

4. Do your employees have a sense of ownership for the team or departmental goals?

5. Does a process exist independent of you to let people know if they are winning or losing?

6. Do your current goals and objectives educate, facilitate and motivate your organization?

7. Is your current goal system a "paperwork drill" in which you spend time compiling, computing, and publishing charts that diagnose performance?

Comment:

Unless employees "get" the connection between their jobs and the company's business goals, they will have a "what's in it for me?" mentality. They must truly see how their performance – regardless of the job – affects the company's overall success.

A simple method to achieve this connectivity is the business scorecard – a sustainable process that will endure long after you are gone.

Chapter 11: Surprise!

Up to this point, Tim had deferred to Ima throughout the plant tour, saying little as she oriented Neuman to his new job. Now, glancing at his watch, he interjected, "We've been at this for a couple hours now. I don't know about you, but I would like to get off my feet for a few minutes. Why don't we head toward the breakroom and get a cup of coffee?"

The breakroom at the Eniware plant was a large, comfortable area where people congregated on their lunch hours and shift breaks. It had vending machines and fresh coffee. Today it had something else.

As Tim pulled open the door for Ima to enter, a roomful of workers all yelled, "Surprise!"

Ima stopped in her tracks and looked around. It appeared as though half the plant — as many that could crowd into the room — had taken over every available table and chair and stood shoulder-to-shoulder around a makeshift stage at the far end of the room. A large banner was stretched over the stage and a king-sized cake rested on a table. Both read, "We'll miss you, Ima!"

Ima stood still, for a moment at a loss for words. Finally she stammered, "What? … When? … I don't know what to say!"

Amid an off-key rendition of "For she's a jolly good fellow!" Tim escorted her to center stage where a trio of chairs and a microphone had been set up.

"You didn't think we'd let you go without saying goodbye, did you?" he asked.

"I … I … I never expected …" stammered Ima.

"Hush, now!" reprimanded Tim. "You'll have your chance to talk later. Right now, other people have some things to say."

The first person to edge forward was Millie, an older woman who worked in the product assembly department. Ima was surprised to see her come to the stage. Millie was a shy person who rarely spoke out. She was the type of individual who easily gets lost in a crowd and fades into the background because she appears to lack the self-confidence to speak up for herself.

Millie stood in front of the microphone, half facing Ima. She cleared her throat and tested the mike. Pulling out her notes, she said in a quiet voice:

"Ima, if you were anybody else, any other plant manager, I'm sure you wouldn't know my name. That's because most people aren't even aware that I am around. Mostly I like that, because I don't like to be the center of attention.

"Factories like Eniware (and I would guess business offices, too) have a lot of employees like me. We go about our business and usually are pretty content just to be left alone. We're quiet, and we're reliable. Most supervisors are happy about that because they know the work gets done and we don't cause any trouble.

"But when you're quiet and don't speak out, supervisors tend not to pay any attention to you — *ever.* They never even tell you when you've done well. The worst thing about being quiet, though, is that people forget that you have ideas and opinions.

"That all changed when you became plant manager, Ima. You started having those team meetings and made it non-negotiable that everyone had to participate — it was 'non-negotiable' as you put it — and that everyone's ideas were valuable. I didn't really think those rules would make any difference, but they did. I'll never forget the day when you sat in on one of my team's first meetings. We were discussing a problem with the quality of the parts that were coming to us. We were getting too many bad parts, and the scrap rate was too high. Everyone was complaining about the problem, but nobody had any ideas on how to solve it.

"Then you asked me for *my* opinion. Me! I couldn't believe it. Because I *did* have an idea on how to solve the problem, and you listened. A lot of managers wouldn't do that. Or if they did ask, it would be like 'lip service' — because they already had in their mind the answer they wanted. Not you. *You asked and you listened.* And my idea was the one that was used. You had it written down on that action register, so I knew you thought it was valuable.

"After that meeting, every time you came into our department, you would stop by my work station and spend a few minutes talking with me. Sometimes you'd just ask how it was going. But just as often, you would ask about me and if I needed anything. And if I had a problem, you would listen — not only with your ears, but with your heart.

"Ima, we are all going to miss you for a lot of different reasons. But I will miss you most because you are a *real* person, with a *real* heart."

Ima brushed aside a tear that had welled up in the corner of her eye. Millie fell back into the crowd and another employee came forward. He was a big, husky guy who didn't look like he would be easily intimidated, just because of his sheer bulk. And it was apparent he wasn't comfortable talking in front of a crowd. He picked up the mike with a reluctant look, then took a deep breath and started talking.

"For those of you who don't know me, I'm Steve. I drive a lift truck. I've done it for more than 10 years. And

I'm good at it. Ask anybody.

"One day — it musta been right after Ima became plant manager — we had an incident. Somehow a batch of sub-quality parts that were supposed to be scrapped was delivered to the assembly department and got used. Fortunately, one of the assembly people caught the mistake — but it wasn't until about half of the parts had been put into the final product. That meant that a whole bunch had to be tested and scrapped — not a nice picture, if you get my meaning. It cost the plant a lotta time and money.

"Of course, the problem got back to Ima fast, and she stormed into the department. I was on my fork truck and she ran up to me and yelled at me for delivering those parts to final assembly. She really blew up! And I admit, we exchanged a few words, which probably could have been chosen better."

Steve glanced at Ima, who recoiled at the memory as the crowd laughed. She nodded faintly. He continued.

"But I gotta give her credit. After she blew up at me, she went off to talk to the supervisor in the parts department. She found out what I had told her all along … *It wasn't my fault.* Someone in the parts department had not labeled the parts as scrap and had placed the bin in the regular pick-up place. There was *no way* I could have known they weren't good! So, after she talked to that supervisor who explained everything, she came back to me — *and apologized.* She said — and I remember every word — 'It was wrong of me to get angry with you and to blame you for the mistake. I should have gotten all the facts before I said anything. And I should *never* have pointed fingers. That's wrong. Mistakes happen. The important thing is that we don't make them again. I'm sorry for getting angry. I hope you will accept my apology.'

"I've had supervisors and managers get mad at me before (and sometimes I deserved it!), but I never had one admit they were wrong. Ima, you may be a foot shorter and a hundred pounds lighter than me, but you're a bigger person."

He put down the mike and sauntered off the stage.

Ima smiled.

Mary, a quality assurance specialist, was up next. Like so many others, Mary had worked at Eniware for a long time. She knew her job inside and out, and you could tell by watching her that she enjoyed it. Some of the most fun she had was crunching numbers to find out if materials, parts, and finished product met customer specifications — and to help troubleshoot problems when tolerances started to trend outside of specs.

Mary spoke directly to Ima. "Ima, one of the things I've always admired about you was the respect you give everybody. If my memory serves me right, we both started here on the same day. Boy, that was a long time ago! You've advanced and made your job a career. I never had career aspirations. I've always just wanted to do a good job. I started on the production line and then got into quality control, where I've been ever since. I guess it'll be where I'll finish when I get ready to retire, which isn't too far behind you!

"Anyway ... a lot of people might look down on me because I'm still in that same job. They might say I didn't have any ambition or I wasn't smart enough to get ahead. But not you! You've always made me feel like I was the most important person in this plant! Like the time when you came to me and asked me to teach you how to do some calculations so you could understand the quality charts better! And that was after you became plant manager. Imagine that … the plant manager coming to me for help! Thank you for that. Thank you for the respect you've always given each of us, no matter what we do."

For the next 20 minutes, the accolades and roasts kept coming. Sitting in her hot seat, Ima was held captive to the lovingly barbed stories her employees kept recounting.

Just when she thought the ordeal was over, one more employee came forward. Ima did a double take when she saw him: It was Monk E. Onurbak.

He climbed on stage and said to Ima:

"I'll bet you're surprised to see me up here. You probably thought I would be jumping for joy because you're leaving Eniware!" He turned to the audience. "Actually, I'm a little surprised myself! It seems that for as long as I can remember, Ima's been a pain in my behind. Or, maybe it was the other way around? …

"A lot of you know that I've been working here for a lotta years, more than I care to remember. When I came to Eniware, I thought I had made it to easy street. Punch a clock, put in a little time, do just enough. That's the way it had always been. They never fired anyone here! Or so I thought. It was 'fun' for a long time," he said amid audience laughter.

"But then they made *her* my supervisor!" He nodded toward Ima.

"At first she wasn't too bad. We still had the run of the roost! As long as we met those production standards, nobody seemed to get on our backs too much.

"But then one day, something happened. The *old* Ima I had come to *tolerate* as a supervisor was replaced by a *new* Ima. That new Ima set down some *non-negotiables* and made it clear that our team was gonna live by them — *or else*. And believe me when I say, it was 'or else.' I know a bunch of people who are not here today because they didn't believe there was an 'or else.'

"*It wasn't just all talk with her.* She put our feet to the fire. I got close enough to that fire to get scorched a few times, and that finally made me realize that each of us had to pull our weight to make the plant and the company successful.

"Don't get me wrong: I've had plenty of supervisors tell me how important work was … yadda yadda yadda. But Ima *showed* us how the work we did affected everything that happened here. If we didn't do our best and work up to expectations, we had to pay the consequences.

"That new Ima always walked the talk. She always held herself to the same rules she held everyone else to. Like … the parking spaces. When she became plant manager, she did away with those reserved spaces for supervisors that were up close to the front door. The early bird gets the worm, she said. She said no one should have special parking spaces — not even her. So she parks where everyone else does, even if that means she has to walk from the back of the parking lot on a cold winter morning. She never pulls rank.

"I gotta admire her for that. I also gotta admire her for standing up and doing the right thing, even when it coulda cost her her job. I heard Steve telling you about the time when Ima apologized to him. What he didn't tell you was the *rest* of the story.

"Those bad parts got mixed up and were used in final product, all right. But the problem started with the raw materials that were used in the parts. They were substandard. On the outside, the final product looked fine. There was no way anybody could have known that it was defective. When Ima found out, she could have let them be shipped. But no. She trashed them. Scrapping that quantity of final product caused us to lose money, and it also caused us to lose time. You know that we're committed to just-in-time delivery. And if we're late, our customer is late, too. Ima risked her job when she made the decision to scrap the product. But she did that instead of risking the quality and reputation of this plant.

"It would have been easier for her to put herself first, but she didn't. But she does the 'next right thing' even if it isn't the most popular thing to do.

"I've been yapping up here long enough, but I just want to say one more thing."

He turned toward Ima. "Ima, even when you were a supervisor, you always told your employees they could come to you for help. A long time ago, I thought that meant you would do what I asked you to do — to fix my problems for me! I learned different.

"I found out that coming to you for help meant learning how to help myself. We've had our differences, but I just wanted to tell you that that was one of the best lessons I ever learned.

"Ima, thank you for all you have given us. Thank you for what you have given me. I may still be a pain in your behind, but it's a much smaller pain today than it was years ago."

Monk left the dais.

Ima couldn't stop the tears from flowing.

Tim beamed with pride.

Lesson 11: Leading with a Heart

After all this talk about the dangers of managing by personality, you may be wondering, "We all have personalities. Are you saying we have to somehow abandon them? Become process gurus and forsake our identity, style, and traits?"

Absolutely not. What we are saying is that your personality and individual style are essential — *once* you establish a process that creates a consistent and stable concentration on business focus, urgency, and accountability.

Process lets you emerge from a 3 P mentality. Without process, egocentric leadership dominates.

Organizations today do not need larger-than-life saviors with magnetic personalities to drive performance.

Many teams today are led by strong leaders with even stronger personalities. These leaders get results, but once these leaders are gone, the team's performance quickly atrophies. Regrettably, too many leaders (3 P leaders) like the feel of strapping on the red cape, swooping in, and saving the day. Although this type of leadership validates their egos, it creates a level of dependency — not accountability. This egocentric, 3 P leadership is devastating for long-term success.

An egocentric model can and does work, but it drives loyalty to the personality, not commitment to the business. The 3 C leadership model, on the other hand, works, because it couples process with heart.

True leadership cannot happen if the leader has no heart.

So, what exactly is a heart-centric leader?

A heart-centric leader is one who channels his ego away from himself and into the larger goal of building a great team. It is not that heart-centric leaders have no ego or self-interest — they are incredibly ambitious — but their ambition is for the team, not themselves.

Heart-centric leaders cultivate a number of personal characteristics, which are as diverse as they are. But if you were to closely analyze the key traits of the top heart-centric leaders you would find five that they likely have in common:

- Humility,
- Passion,
- Stewardship,
- Integrity, and
- Vision.

Let's take a closer look at each of these and see how they are personified in 3 C leaders.

Humility
Humility is an often misunderstood term. Some people interpret humility to mean that a person must never say good things about himself, never take pride in his work, and always defer to others.

Nothing could be farther from the truth.

A humble leader:
• **Is one who is unpretentious and modest.** It is someone who believes (and acts on that belief) that he no better than anyone else. He is genuine, in a heartfelt way. He does not seek hero or celebrity status.

• **Has a deep sense of self-awareness, not self-importance.** These two phrases — self-awareness and self-importance — sound similar but are absolutely opposite in application.

A person who purports self-importance uses many "I" statements, such as, " I did…", "I accomplished…," "I created…"

"I" statements are audible indications of the leader's singular belief that the event or accomplishment occurred only because of him. These statements also imply an utter disregard for the input of others — their contributions, intelligence, knowledge, and skills.

In contrast, a sense of *self-awareness* implies that the individual knows his strengths and the limitations of those strengths. He also understands his weaknesses and their consequences and acknowledges these weaknesses, so that he can work toward defeating — or at least minimizing — them.

A deep sense of self-awareness is driven by the "I am not nor will I ever be perfect" belief. Many people readily admit their imperfections, particularly when they justify their behavior or less-than-stellar performance. They say, "I admit I made a mistake. After all, I'm not perfect!" Yet these same people, through their use of "I" statements, continue to point to a different perception of themselves.

Self-awareness relies on feedback and the constant, sincere search for both facts and perceptions. Self-awareness is not defensive.

Self-awareness springs from sincere humility. Self-awareness can only be achieved if the leader is humble.

• **Stands up for his beliefs.** But, he accepts legitimate authority and is guided by a moral compass.

If you were to survey the best leaders in business today to determine what drives them to become even better, you would often find they are guided by a higher moral compass. They hold true to certain beliefs which they refuse to compromise.

That moral compass may be a question, similar to the one the president of a large carpet manufacturing company is known to ask. When confronted with difficult decisions, he reflects, "What would Jesus do…" as a barometer to assist him in making decisions.

The WWJD (What Would Jesus Do) question is particularly helpful to leaders who want to apply a greater purpose and barometer to decision making, The simple act of asking the question challenges leaders to think beyond the immediacy of the issue and to apply a durable and timeless perspective. As important, the sheer comparative format of the question implies an inherit value-based decision making approach that's missing in many organizations today.

Your moral compass may not be "WWJD." It may be another simple question, such as, "Would I be proud to tell my daughter or son about this?" or "Would I want this on my epitaph?" The idea is that your moral compass allows you to check your motives before you act.

Find your moral compass. Checking whatever compass you use will permit you to remain true to yourself.

• **Does not show jealousy or envy.** Rather, he relishes the accomplishments of others. He channels his ego away from himself and into the larger goal of building an effective organization. The humble person achieves greatest personal satisfaction from witnessing the accomplishments of others.

He validates himself through the successes of the individuals he mentors.

• **Steps back, so that others may go first.** He does not try to be first in all things, because he realizes that being first is not important. Seeing to the needs of others is important.

The simplest gestures often speak volumes about the nature of leaders. *For example:* What can you assume about a leader, who, at a lunch break in a seminar, breaks into line before his staff? That small action tells much about the person — that he thinks more about his needs than those of his employees.

On the other hand, what can you infer about the leader who, in the same situation, waits until everyone has been served before he gets into line? That leader puts others first. This is a simple act, but it speaks volumes about the leader's humility.

• **Meets others more than halfway.** He strives to mediate conflict, find common ground, and resolve differences. He recognizes that win-win solutions are necessary to accomplish great things.

This leader knows that decisions made from an authoritarian position will be implemented but are rarely embraced. He understands that compromise takes careful listening and much patience. And he knows that acknowledgement of an alternative point of view does not compromise position or ego.

He seeks results but relies on a collaborative methodology to achieve those results. He understands the concept of winners and losers. He is gracious in victory and defeat but is never comfortable accepting the alternative ending.

The humble leader acknowledges that give-and-take, ebb-and-flow, are the way of the world and to master this balance is key to his leadership and his being.

• **Is at peace with himself.** He goes home in the evening and is able to sleep, knowing that he has done "the next right thing."

Peace in our hectic lives is a state many people rarely experience. It feels temporary and fleeting. Peace is unattainable to individuals who do not have a core belief system.

A strong leader once said he finally achieved a level of peace with himself and his organization when one day he read a bumper sticker that said, "Let go and let God." Approximately 85 percent of Americans openly state they are Christians and they believe in a higher authority.

Regardless of your spiritual preferences, it cannot be disputed that a common element of heart-centric leadership is peace.

Those leaders successful enough to achieve a heart-centric persona openly recognize they *alone* cannot achieve a peaceful state of being. They rely on some type of higher power.

Do you have peace in your life? Are you trying through your own sheer will and determination to "fix" everything? Leaders who operate this way are physically, emotionally, and spiritually exhausted. They are *not* at peace.

But those who are able to let go because they know they have done the best they can, that they have done the "next right thing," can rest easily at night.

In the workplace: A leader who cultivates the trait of humility sincerely praises the accomplishments of others — peers, superiors, and employees. He never looks down on others even though he may be "above" them in rank or because he has more training or education.

He asks for help in solving workplace problems, because he knows he does not have all the answers. And he wants to hear what others have to say, because he understands that a diversity of opinions can only contribute to a better solution.

When others give him answers, he listens — really listens. He is not caught up in self-importance that would cause him to interrupt and inject his own thoughts at the expense of someone else's.

When he is criticized (by peers, superiors, or even subordinates), he does not cringe or argue. Instead, he takes the criticism, weighs its merits, and acts on it appropriately. Sometimes that means saying, "I'm sorry" or "You are right."

If his boss makes a decision he does not agree with, he may voice his opinion, but he defers to the authority, and he doesn't complain about the decision to others, especially his employees.

When confronted with problems, he tries to find mutually agreeable solutions. He does not give lip service to compromise and acceptance; he lives these values.

A humble leader takes pride in his accomplishments, but acknowledges and values that those accomplishments are the result of teamwork, not his work alone.

Employees who have the fortune to work with a humble leader believe him, trust him, and respect him, because they know he has the business and their well-being at heart.

What are you doing to set your team up for success after you leave? Are you searching for someone like you or more importantly, someone better than you?

Passion

Does passion have a place at work? We think so. In fact, we believe that passion must be part of the emotional makeup of heart-centric, 3 C leaders. Their passion extends from their heart to their work and the people who help them accomplish the business of the company. It drives them to success.

A passionate leader:
• **Has a fierce resolve toward life, people, work, and community.** This leader doesn't let go. She wants the best and is not satisfied until she gets it.
• **Is relentless.** She doesn't stop seeking the best for her team and the organization. She is compelled to carry on — not out of a need to satisfy her ego, but out of need to make the team flourish and the people within the team grow and mature.
Nothing deters her from following her passion. She seeks the reward of seeing the team flourish and the people within the team grow and mature.
A passionate leader who is relentless is not complacent. Rather, she believes she can learn something new each day to advance her passion and commitment to excellence.
• **Is intensely curious.** She wants to know all she can about the things that drive her. She explores to find answers and is not satisfied until she understands. She values the gift of knowledge that has been given to her.
Her curiosity causes her to be a voracious reader who thrives on exploration. She uses knowledge to help her organization make better decisions, not to set herself up as a know-it-all.
• **Is inspirational.** Passionate leaders come in different personality types — shy and introverted, outgoing and extroverted. Regardless of her innate personality style, a passionate leader inspires.
It's important to understand the significant difference between having the ability to be exciting and having the ability to inspire.

Many 3 P leaders feel they must put excitement into their presence and their speech. They are attached more to charisma than to content when they attempt to lead others. These egocentric leaders rely on personality to carry the day.

What they fail to realize is that the ability to inspire does not require theatrics, stage shows, bright lights, or drama. What it requires is the ability and willingness to tell a story. Inspirational leaders tell stories about themselves and send a message to others through their own life experiences. They share their personal growth, including the mistakes they have made and the lessons they have learned.

Leaders who inspire open a door to the past, the present, and the future, and they invite their audience in. They do this by making their listeners personally feel their stories.

A passionate leader understands that the ability to inspire does not require "props;" rather, it requires humility and genuineness.

• **Puts to use her natural talents and skills.** She recognizes that these talents are gifts that must be used, and that everyone around her has talents as well.

• **Surrounds herself with talent.** Leaders who lack humility and a sense of self feel threatened by subordinates and peers who are smart, knowledgeable, and effective. Their egocentric personalities require them to be "top dog." But meeting that personal ego requirement is defeating to the organization.

Effective leaders know better. They surround themselves with people who are smarter than they are. They put aside their own egos and think in terms of the needs of the organization or team. They know that the sum is greater than the whole, and the stronger the individual parts, the stronger the whole.

Passion for the good of the organization is the compelling force behind surrounding themselves with competent people. And passion for the organization allows these leaders to put aside their own egos and make sure they tell their employees how much they value the talents they have.

In the workplace: You know a passionate leader when you meet one.

For example: When a passionate leader talks to a stranger about her work, the stranger comments, "You really like what you do. I can hear it in your voice. I can see it in your face!"

At work, that passion — that enthusiasm — are contagious. When this leader walks into the room, she energizes it and the people with whom she works. They can feel her belief and her desire to do the best job possible. It is impossible not to be touched by her zeal.

She's good at her job. That's because she learns as much as she can in a never-ending search for knowledge. She then applies what she has learned. When problems arise (as they will, either with people or with things), she stays with it; she is committed to the end. She does not quit just because the "going gets tough."

The passion she feels for her work and the people she works with is real; it is not "put on" to satisfy a new workplace program or to advance her career. She is compelled to follow her calling because it is an innate part of her.

Employees who have the fortune to work with a passionate leader want to follow that leader. Her passion is so genuine, it is contagious. It comes from the heart.

Vision

Leaders who "do for others what they are capable of doing for themselves" have what we call a "dumpster mentality."

You know what a dumpster is: It is a commercial trash and garbage receptacle found behind most businesses. Into it go all the discards from the office building.

A management dumpster is the emotional equivalent to a commercial dumpster. It's a mental trash bin for managers. A management dumpster accepts all type of workplace garbage — employee complaints, problems, discarded programs, and the whining of employees, suppliers, and even bosses.

As long as a management dumpster gets emptied regularly, no problems arise. But if it doesn't, then the owner of the dumpster has a big problem to deal with. And all he can see is "stuff" that makes his life miserable.

The problem with a dumpster mentality is that it creates a reactionary focus on yesterday's issues, and does not allow a vision to develop to deal with the challenges of tomorrow.

For the last 10 years, much has been written about strategy and vision and the need for the leaders of organizations to build strategy around vision in order to take their organizations to successful heights.

However, if leaders are buried alive in the issues of yesterday, how can they possibly think about tomorrow? And if they cannot think about tomorrow, creating a "vision" is an exercise in futility.

A heart-centric leader with vision:
- **Must be able to get out of the dumpster.**
Management dumpsters are created largely because of an egocentric, 3 P leadership mentality.

The dumpster and its managing-by-personality premises create a culture of selective engagement, in which employees are less than committed to the business of the organization.

The first step in solving any problem is to acknowledge it. Visionary leaders must acknowledge the current culture of selective engagement, deal with it by putting Process-Based Leadership™ into place, and move the organization toward a culture of collective accountability.

Visionary leaders ensure visibility of accountability throughout the team. It is through this accountability that engagement is achieved. And it is through this accountability that all members of the team become maximally engaged in the running of the business.

- **Is not enamored by vague notions of empowerment.**
A visionary leader understands empowerment to be the expedient deployment of responsibilities that were not performed yesterday, but — through education, coaching, and belief — can be performed tomorrow.

He recognizes that empowerment is not simply a vague feeling or emotion, but is the demonstration of confidence of leaders to their people.

Lastly, he understands that empowerment must be backed up by real deliverables that drive the business.

- **Is able to tell a story that has three components.** The components are *yesterday* ("Where have we come from?"), *today* ("Why are we here and how does it feel?"), and *tomorrow* ("Where are we going and why do I need you to go with me?")

To tell this story, the leader doesn't have to be a dynamic orator. Nor does he need to embellish his story. He just needs to tell it from the perspective of someone who is on a journey and believes that journey is best traveled when accompanied by companions.

• **Is optimistic. Vision requires optimism.** When optimism prevails, adversity cannot have the last word.

A visionary leader inspires optimism.

He is able to convey, in the midst of complacency or tragedy, the belief that tomorrow will be better and that each person possesses the ability to succeed.

He is able to channel the message that the team's experience is not in vain; its responses are not futile; and its efforts will be worthwhile.

The heart-centric visionary leader must be able to point to a place on the horizon — a shining city on the mountain — that serves to ground his people on where they are going, so that personality, position, and persuasion do not take them in the wrong direction.

In the workplace:

The visionary leader puts into place a basic process that focuses on accountability to the business and holds every person in the organization to that accountability. By making people accountable for the business, the leader aims them toward the future, not on the past.

The visionary leader speaks from his heart when he addresses employees. He shares his experience, strength, and hope, to clear away the fog of the past and clearly see the future, which he can present in clear detail.

Employees who have the fortune to work with a visionary leader want to go where that leader is going. His vision is clear. And that clarity begets loyalty and commitment.

Stewardship
Stewardship, in its basic meaning, is the assumption of personal responsibility for taking care of something that is not your own.

A heart-centric leader is a steward of her organization. She is entrusted with serving the needs of the organization and her employees. In other words, she does not assume a leadership position to meet her own needs; rather, she takes it on to fulfill the needs of those around her.

That does not mean, of course, that she takes over the responsibilities of her employees. Rather, it means that she assumes a deep responsibility to help her employees and her organization succeed.

So, what does it mean to be a steward of the organization?

A heart-centric leader who is a steward:

• **Treats employees as her best customers.** Think about the last time you were treated as a "best customer" — perhaps at an elegant restaurant:

The maitre d' accompanied you to your table, pulled out your chair, placed the napkin in your lap, and made you feel as though you were his only guests.

The server asked if you had any special dietary needs, carefully explained each item on the menu, and recommended items he thought you would like.

When the meal was served, the bread basket and water glasses were always full. The serving staff stood in the background and saw to your unvoiced needs.

If there was a problem with the meal — an undercooked steak or an overcooked fish or something you expected to like but did not — you were given a replacement along with a sincere apology.

And at the end of the meal, the servers thanked you graciously for joining them for the evening.

How good did you feel?

The server was a steward. He anticipated and accommodated your needs but did not overstep his boundaries.

The heart-centric leader is such a steward to her employees. She watches over them to make sure they have he tools, skills, knowledge, and equipment — and the empowerment — to do the business of the company.

At the same time, she anticipates and accommodates the needs of the business — by envisioning the future, planning, and strategizing how to make the company successful.

To the heart-centric leader, employees and the company *are* her best customers. And they know it.

• **Shepherds the character of her employees.** A shepherd is a person who guards or watches over others so that no harm can come to them.

Egocentric, 3 P leaders focus on taking care of their own needs over those of anyone else. Their self-centeredness rubs off on employees, who begin to care only for "What's in it for me?" instead of "How can I help make the business more successful?"

A 3 C, heart-centric leader who is a steward to her employees and organization, on the other hand, reigns in the tendency of employees to satisfy their own needs at the expense of the company's. She shapes and tends to the character of her employees and focuses them on the greater good for the whole of the organization — by empowering them and making them visibly accountable.

• **Knows what's important to her people.** A leader who embraces the trait of stewardship knows the top two most important things of each employee on her team. She knows these things because she talks to her employees and listens to what they have to say.

The talk is not always centered on work. She is not naïve to think that work is the most important thing in the lives of her workers. So, she listens to them discuss their goals, their future, their families, their leisure time activities — the drivers in their lives.

And she inquires about these things — not because making inquiries is required of her as a leader, but because she genuinely cares and is interested.

To this steward, showing genuine interest is not a responsibility; it is an honor.

• **Teaches her team to be self-sufficient.** An old Chinese proverb says, "Give a man a fish, and you feed him for a day. Teach a man to fish, and you feed him for a lifetime."

A heart-centric leader teaches her employees to be self-sufficient, because in this way, they can succeed even when she is not there. She does not want them to rely on her; she wants them to rely on themselves. She teaches self-sufficiency by providing the means for visible accountability.

Although initially some employees may think that responsibility (accountability) is shackling, the heart-centric leader demonstrates to them that accountability is actually freeing. The more accountability they accept, the freer they become, because they always know where they stand and where to go next.

• **Allows failure to happen.** You have most certainly heard the expressions, "no pain, no gain" and "the pain of learning." These two adages express a truism: No one learns until he *needs* to learn. And he feels the need to learn when the current situation hurts too much.

Although a steward protects her people, her protection does not extend to saving them from learning experiences. No one wants to fail, but failure (pain) is the way in which learning occurs.

A steward leader looks at failure as an opportunity to teach her people success. She does not place blame for the failure; rather, she helps her people see how to avoid the failure the next time around.

• **Shows a strong sense of ethical concern.** To care for, to oversee, and to protect: These are concepts that are not easily embraced or understood by egocentric 3 P leaders, but they are fundamental to heart-centric 3 C leaders.

The heart-centric leader understands that although a passion for results is paramount, equally important is a passion for the care and nurturing of her people. She balances these two with a sense of serving both.

In the workplace:
Frequently we ask organizations about how they demonstrate awareness and appreciation for their people assets. We regularly hear variations of the same answer — recognition, rewards, and praise.

As worthy as these things are, each falls back on one (if not all) of the 3 P's — position, proximity, or persuasion. Why? Because recognition, rewards, and praise rely on the personality of the leader to achieve the desired goal.

Heart-centric stewardship demands more than recognition and reward programs. A heart-centric steward has personal conversations with employees to let them know they are valued and appreciated and to help them become more than they thought they could be.

The heart-centric steward empowers her employees and holds them accountable, so that they can learn through failure as well as success.

Many large companies have adopted succession-planning programs as tools to help their leaders talk to employees about aspirations and help these aspirations become real. Succession planning — or better stated, succession growing — is something that all companies can do to prepare themselves and their employees for the future. This type of growing is an act of stewardship.

Employees who are fortunate enough to have a leader who is a heart-centric steward trust their leader, and through that trust, they learn to accept responsibility and to grow to their fullest potential.

Integrity
None of us is promised a life without adversity. How we deal with adversity is one measure of our integrity.

Ironic as it may seem, another measure of integrity is how we deal with success. Temptations associated with success have been the undoing of many egocentric leaders. Once they taste success, they believe they can do anything and that they are above the laws (legal or moral) that apply to everyone else.

Of the five traits consistently found in heart-centric leaders, integrity is the one that binds them all together. It is the character trait that causes us to do the next right thing.

Integrity is that core set of values against which decisions are measured. Integrity drives consistency — one of the 3 C's.

Integrity is the foundation of principled leadership.

A heart-centric leader whose leadership is based on integrity:
• **Is ethical and honorable.** Although he faces tough decisions, he does the next right thing. He does not bow to pressure, but follows his heart, guided by his moral compass. That compass may be the simple question, "What would Jesus do?" as we discussed earlier. Or, perhaps, "Would I be proud to tell my daughter or son about this?"

An ethical and honorable leader does not have to look over his shoulder to see if anyone is watching; he acts as if the whole world sees his every move — and does not care, because he is true to himself.

An honorable and ethical leader has no problem sleeping at night because of the decisions he has made during the day.

• **Is uncorrupted.** When a database maintains its integrity, it is said to be uncorrupted. The same can apply to a leader. When a heart-centric leader maintains his integrity, he remains uncorrupted — "pure," as it were, to his principles.

• **Understands the importance of straight talk.** Integrity is all about straight talk — not the type of straight talk that justifies poor behavior and rudeness, but the type of straight talk that clearly articulates the situation, behavior, and impact (SBI). This SBI-modeled straight-talk gives leaders the ability to confront barriers and obstacles head on.

Heart-centric leaders recognize the value of critical conversations and additionally see conflict as necessary and healthy, but, if avoided, disastrous.

• **Holds true to his commitments.** When a person accepts a leadership role, he commits to doing right by the organization and his people. A heart-centric leader holds true to that commitment, even when the going gets tough. He understands that when wealth is lost, *nothing* is lost. When health is lost, something is lost. But when character is lost, *everything* is lost.

In the workplace:
Upper-level leaders often must make difficult decisions. An egocentric 3 P leader might make a decision by stating, "It isn't illegal, so we will do it."

A heart-centric 3 C leader, acting on his integrity, would look at the same situation and say, "If I have to ask if it is illegal, then it is unethical. I will not do it."

All leaders, regardless of their level in the organization, are on occasion faced with the same type of decision. A leader who acts with integrity does the right thing, based on his principles: He doesn't allow questionable product to be sent to customers; he does not allow employees who fail to be accountable to remain on the team.

A heart-centric leader keeps his commitments — not only to the organization, but to his employees. He holds himself visibly accountable, just as he holds his employees. He teaches commitment by being committed.

This leader does not mince words. He talks straight, to his employees as well as to his superiors, focusing on the situation, behavior and impact — because straight talk is honest talk. He expects the same from his employees.

He understands that the farther a leader climbs up the corporate ladder, the harder it is to receive honest feedback. Therefore, he makes it easier for his employees to give him feedback.

Employees who are fortunate enough to work for a heart-centric leader with integrity always know where they stand and trust their leader to be consistent and clear in his expectations for performance and success.

We could list more qualities that heart-centric leaders carry into the workplace. But the five essential ones — *humility, passion, vision, stewardship,* and *integrity* — are those that comprise the core of a heart-centric, 3 C leader.

These traits, combined with sustainable business processes that drive clarity, consistency, and connectivity — are the keys to leaving a leadership legacy.

Legacy leadership requires you to have heart, with a business focus.

Self-Assessment 11: Are You a Heart-Centric Leader?

Humility

1.   Would your employees say you are (a) genuine or (b) pretentious?

2.   Take note of your vocabulary: Do you use "I" and "me" or "We" and "us"? If you find yourself using more "I" statements, what steps can you take to change the "I's" to "We's"?

3.   Do you have a moral compass? What is it?

4.   How do you show respect to your employees: Do you give them credit for the work they have done — not only by praising them in front of their peers, but also by passing their accomplishments upward to make upper management aware of them?

5.   Do you say you are sorry — even to your employees — when you are wrong?

6.   Do you get more pleasure out of your own accomplishments or those of your employees? If it is the former, what steps can you take to develop your interest in the accomplishments of your employees?

7.   When you are at a seminar luncheon, do you expect to be served first, or do you make sure everyone else is taken care of before you eat?

8.   Do you give credit when and where credit is due?

9.   Do you exaggerate your experiences to make yourself appear prominent and important? If so, what can you do to minimize this tendency?

10. Do you begin thinking about your next assignment within weeks of assuming your current assignment? If so, what steps can you take to remain focused on the doing the best job today, which will pave the way for your next assignment?

Passion

11. When you talk to a stranger about what you do, does the stranger feel your passion?

12. Are you driven to do your best *always?*

13. Do your employees walk away from a conversation with you feeling inspired? Do they catch your enthusiasm?

14. When employees look at you, do they see an optimistic leader, even under challenging circumstances?

15. Are you a sincere story teller? Do you share your experience, strength, and hope with listeners to inspire them to higher levels?

16. Do you surround yourself with talented people and tap into those talents?

Vision

17. Have you escaped from the dumpster of tried-and-failed programs and complaints of employees, suppliers, and superiors?

18. Do you empower your employees to deliver outcomes?

19. Do you have ideas about the future of the organization? Do you share your vision with your employees to help them connect with it? Or are you so consumed with meeting short-term goals (perhaps to earn a bonus or incentive) that you have not thought about the organization's future?

20. Do you call upon your employees to help shape your ideas for the future of the organization — and then credit them with the successes they help achieve?

21. When you tell stories, do you talk about yesterday, today, and tomorrow?

Stewardship

22. Have you risen to a leadership role because you wanted power and authority, or because you truly felt you could influence the organization?

23. Do you treat your employees as your best customers?

24. Do you know the things that are most important to each of your employees? When was the last time you talked with each of them about what was important to them?

25. Do you really listen to employees when they talk to you?

26. Have you put into place processes by which you can "hear" employees even when you cannot talk with them face-to-face?

27. The last time your team had a failure, what did you do?

Integrity

28. When you make a personal promise, do you always keep it?

29. When you make promises to your employees, do you always keep them?

30. Do you hold yourself accountable to the same rules and expectations to which you hold your employees?

31. Have you put into place processes, such as action registers and team handbooks, which allow the organization to document mistakes and take corrective action, so they won't be repeated in the future?

Integrity

28. When you make a personal promise, do you always keep it?

29. When you make promises to your employees, do you always keep them?

30. Do you hold yourself accountable to the same rules and expectations to which you hold your employees?

31. Have you put into place processes, such as action registers and team handbooks, which allow the organization to document mistakes and take corrective action, so they won't be repeated in the future?

Comment:

As you answered the heart-centric questions, you may have felt an objection stir within you: *I would really like to demonstrate my heart-centric qualities, but I just don't have time.*

Heart-centric characteristics can be enhanced only if you are confident of stability in achieving day-to-day objectives. If you are leading by the 3 P's, your heart-centric qualities will never be exposed.

The 3 C's — clarity, consistency, and connectivity — tend to bring out great heart-centric leadership traits. At the same time, great leaders who have these heart-centric traits recognize the value of putting into place self-sustaining processes that drive clarity, consistency, and connectivity to achieve among their workforce a true degree of focus, urgency, and accountability.

Heart-centric leaders who lead by the 3 C's leave a leadership legacy.

Chapter 12: The Pledge

As Monk stepped down from the dais, Neuman whispered something in Tim's ear. Tim nodded and motioned toward the microphone.

"I'm Neuman Lerner. Once Ima officially hands over the keys to the plant, they tell me I'll be your new plant manager," he smiled as he introduced himself.

"I met some of you earlier today when Ima and Tim Leder took me on a tour of the plant. And I'm looking forward to meeting and knowing each and every one of you.

"I realize that this isn't a welcome party for me; it's a thank-you party for Ima, for all she has given to you throughout her years at Eniware. But I felt a real need to tell you about some things I learned today, because they speak so well of Ima Manijer.

"When I was offered this position – taking over Ima's job – before I accepted, I did a lot of homework. I studied up on Eniware, because I wanted to understand what my work would be when I got here.

"I have to tell you, I came away from my homework really impressed! This is a great place! All of you are to be commended. The quality of your work, the amount of work you do … it's great.

"But my homework left me with some very big questions: *How does this plant consistently come out on top? Why are your customer satisfaction ratings so high? Why are scrap costs so low? Why is turnover of employees almost negligible?*

"My tour this morning – and this roast – helped answer those questions.

"Accountability in action. That's the answer. Everyone

– you, your supervisors, and your managers – takes personal responsibility for making this plant shine. You take pride in your work. And it really shows, just in case you don't know it.

"On the tour today I saw real teamwork. Not the textbook kind of teamwork that consultants talk about, but the kind of teamwork that comes from people who really care about each other and what they're doing. Teamwork tied together through non-negotiable processes. You do what you need to do because you *know* what needs to be done. And you know what needs to be done because you see how each person's work helps the plant succeed.

"*How* do you know? Those home team meetings Ima started have a lot to do with that, I would guess. Getting the scoop from your team leader who gets it from the plant manager. The communication system here is absolutely great.

"Of course, talk is cheap. Unless you have tools to do the job, you can't do much. But Ima has also given you tools, such as the team handbook, action registers, and most importantly, business scorecards. These tools give the right amount of discipline and consistency to your workplace, and they connect you with the overall goals of the plant and the company. What a process! What a system!

"But there is something else in this plant. Something very important. The consistency, clarity, and connectivity you have here are all held together by a robust process that allows leaders to use their talents, traits, and styles where they are most needed, and that is to motivate and inspire.

"I think one great thing Ima is leaving behind – and that I intend to carry on – is this: *We are all here to help each other succeed.*

"To all of you — and to you, Ima — I make this pledge: 'If it ain't broke, don't fix it.' The plant is not broken. Far from it, it works extremely effectively. What Ima has put into place will stay in place. Her leadership is a true legacy."

Neuman put the microphone down and stepped back. The room broke into a spontaneous chorus: "Speech! Speech!" They yelled.

Ima wiped away tears. Tim held the microphone out to her. She got up from her chair.

"I … I … don't know what to say!" she stammered. "This party came as a complete surprise. I never saw it coming!

"And then this 'roast' … Listening to you … I never knew that's how you felt." She glowed from embarrassment and delight.

"The only thing I can really say is 'thank you.' You will never know how much this surprise means to me."

The employees of Eniware might not know, but Tim did. Now she knows, he thought. He smiled to her as he handed her the knife to cut the cake.

Lesson 12: Leaving the Legacy

If you left your organization, were promoted or retired today, what would you leave behind?

So many times, we look forward to the future, but we forget about our obligations to the present.

As leaders, we have a moral obligation to leave our teams and organizations with a process that lives beyond our physical presence. This process must give our employees stability, certainty, and confidence. It must be a process that is not dependent on our proximity, our persuasive abilities, or our position. As we have learned, the remnants of these 3 Ps are temporary and fleeting.

Our obligation as leaders is to build and deploy a system that is both visible and auditable that drives the 3 Cs of clarity, consistency, and connectivity and institutionalizes itself as the "way we do business," regardless of personality. This is truly the path to leaving a leadership legacy.

Self-Assessment 12: Your Legacy

1. Have you put into place processes that will focus the workforce whether or not you are present?

2. Are the processes that you have put into place visible to everyone and auditable – characteristics that make them self-sustaining?

3. Describe these processes.

4. What will your leadership legacy be?

Comment:

Legacies are not built in a day. But to start building a legacy, you must start today. It is never too late to have a new beginning.

Chapter 13: The Legacy Lives

The employees of the Eniware plant came forward to claim their cake and give Ima warm hugs and congratulations. Each expressed how much they would miss her. A few old timers lingered to reminisce. And the younger ones, who had never known the "old" Ima, quizzed their seniors for more details about the stories they heard during the roast.

After a while, the celebration began to wind down. People stole glances at the clock and pulled themselves away to get back to work.

Finally, the only people left in the large breakroom were Ima, Tim, and Neuman.

Neuman said, "That was really some party. Were you really surprised, Ima?"

"Surprised? I never had a clue ... And the things they said. I think they really meant them! And Neuman ... thank you for what you said. You will do well here." She shook his hand warmly.

The three managers walked slowly to the door. Tim stopped and looked at Ima. "Now do you see, Ima? You can go on with your life, because you have left a true legacy – a legacy of leadership that will continue unabated because it lives in each individual. You gave them confidence and inspiration. And most importantly, you gave them the ability to make an impact."

Ima smiled and nodded. "Yes, I think I can."

The three managers sat in silence for a few minutes, when suddenly the stillness was broken by the ringing of

Ima's cell phone. She flipped the phone open, and said:

"Yes, Mr. Mayor. It's true. I *am* retiring from the Eniware Manufacturing Plant. ... Would I be available to help you? How? ... The director of sanitation just resigned and the team is lost and doesn't know what it should do? I know just what they need ..."

Chapter 14: A Final Comment

What are your thoughts right now as you finish reading *Leaving Your Leadership Legacy*?

Are you inspired because you realize you created systems that give your team the proper clarity, consistency, and connectivity to lead them to sustained success?

Or are you discouraged because the descriptions of position, proximity, and persuasion accurately reflect your current leadership style?

We hope you relate more to the former than the latter. However, if you see yourself as leading by the 3 Ps, don't despair: The beauty of a legacy is that you still have time to establish it and refine it.

You have the answers in your hand. This book has afforded you many visible and auditable systems to challenge your thinking and your leading.

The processes are important, but just as important (or perhaps more so) is your heart. If you were to eavesdrop on your employees, would you hear them describe you and your leadership as the employees described Ima in Chapter 11? Would they use words like *humility, visionary, stewardship and integrity, fair, passionate, respectful, and genuine* in context with your name?

Never forget that heart-centric qualities are required for a leader to leave a legacy. Cultivate these qualities as you put into place sustainable processes, and you *will* leave a legacy.

Legacies aren't about tomorrow. They are about *now*.

What will your leadership legacy be?

If you found this book helpful, you will want to read these, also by the leaders of Competitive Solutions:

ISBN 1-892538-15-6

This is the book that taught Ima Manijer the process-based management system she needed to climb out of the dumpster and create an outstanding leadership legacy.

This book reveals techniques that resulted in an increase in revenue of 120 percent at a business unit of Nortel, based on ten principles of "UnManagement"

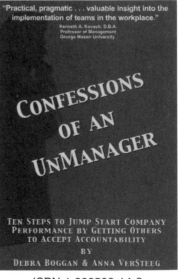

ISBN 1-892538-14-8

Visit LeanTransformation.com or call 1-800-295-4066, M-F 9-5 Eastern